SHEPHERD'S NOTES

Shepherd's Notes Titles Available

SHEPHERD'S NOTES COMMENTARY SERIES

Old Testament

0-80549-028-0	Genesis	0-80549-341-7	Psalms 101-150
0-80549-056-6	Exodus	0-80549-016-7	Proverbs
0-80549-069-8	Leviticus & Numbers	0-80549-059-0	Ecclesiastes, Song of
0-80549-027-2	Deuteronomy		Solomon
0-80549-058-2	Joshua & Judges	0-80549-197-X	Isaiah
0-80549-057-4	Ruth & Esther	0-80549-070-1	Jeremiah-
0-80549-063-9	1 & 2 Samuel		Lamentations
0-80549-007-8	1 & 2 Kings	0-80549-078-7	Ezekiel
0-80549-064-7	1 & 2 Chronicles	0-80549-015-9	Daniel
0-80549-194-5	Ezra, Nehemiah	0-80549-326-3	Hosea-Obadiah
0-80549-006-X	Job	0-80549-334-4	Jonah-Zephaniah
0-80549-339-5	Psalms 1-50	0-80549-065-5	Haggai-Malachi
0-80549-340-9	Psalms 51-100		

New Testament

1-55819-688-9	Matthew	1-55819-689-7	Philippians,
0-80549-071-X	Mark		Colossians, &
0-80549-004-3	Luke		Philemon
1-55819-693-5	John	0-80549-000-0	1 & 2 Thessalonians
1-55819-691-9	Acts	1-55819-692-7	1 & 2 Timothy, Titus
0-80549-005-1	Romans	0-80549-336-0	Hebrews
0-80549-325-5	1 Corinthians	0-80549-018-3	James
0-80549-335-2	2 Corinthians	0-80549-019-1	1 & 2 Peter & Jude
1-55819-690-0	Galatians	0-80549-214-3	1, 2 & 3 John
0-80549-327-1	Ephesians	0-80549-017-5	Revelation

SHEPHERD'S NOTES CHRISTIAN CLASSICS

0-80549-347-6	Mere Christianity-C.S.Lewis	0-80549-394-8	Miracles-C.S.Lewis
0-80549-353-0	The Problem of Pain/ A Grief Observed-C.S.Lewis	0-80549-196-1	Lectures to My Students-Charles Haddon Spurgeon
0-80549-199-6	The Confessions-Augustine	0-80549-220-8	The Writings of Justin Martyr
0-80549-200-3	Calvin1s Institutes	0-80549-345-X	The City of God

SHEPHERD'S NOTES-BIBLE SUMMARY SERIES

0-80549-377-8	Old Testament	0-80549-385-9	Life & Letters of Paul
0-80549-378-6	New Testament	0-80549-376-X	Manners & Customs of Bible Times
0-80549-384-0	Life & Teachings of Jesus	0-80549-380-8	Basic Christian Beliefs

SHEPHERD'S NOTES

When you need a guide through the Scriptures

Acts

HOLMAN
REFERENCE

Nashville, Tennessee

Dewey Decimal Classification: 226.6
Subject Heading: BIBLE. N.T. ACTS
Library of Congress Card Catalog Number: 97–25034

Library of Congress Cataloging-in-Publication Data
Acts / Dana Gould, editor
     p. cm.—(Shepherd's notes)
    Includes bibliographical references.
    ISBN 1–55819–691–9 (tp)
    1. Bible. N.T. Acts—Study and teaching.   I. Gould, Dana,
1951–.   II. Series.
  BS2626.A33   1997
  226.6'0071—DC21   97–25034
                                       CIP

10 11 12 07 06 05

CONTENTS

FOREWORD

Dear Reader:

Shepherd's Notes are designed to give you a quick, step-by-step overview of every book of the Bible. They are not meant to be a substitute for the biblical text; rather, they are study guides intended to help you explore the wisdom of Scripture in personal or group study and to apply that wisdom successfully in your own life.

Shepherd's Notes guide you through both the main themes of each book of the Bible and illuminate fascinating details through appropriate commentary and reference notes. Historical and cultural background information brings the Bible into sharper focus.

Six different icons, used throughout the series, call your attention to historical-cultural information, Old Testament and New Testament references, word pictures, unit summaries, and personal application for everyday life.

Whether you are a novice or a veteran at Bible study, I believe you will find *Shepherd's Notes* a resource that will take you to a new level in your mining and applying the riches of Scripture.

In Him,

David R. Shepherd
Editor-in-Chief

DESIGNED FOR THE BUSY USER

Shepherd's Notes for *Acts* is designed to provide an easy-to-use tool for getting a quick handle on a Bible book's important features, and for gaining an understanding of the message of Acts. Information available in more difficult-to-use reference works has been incorporated into the *Shepherd's Notes* format. This brings you the benefits of many more advanced and expensive works packed into one small volume.

Shepherd's Notes are for laymen, pastors, teachers, small-group leaders and participants, as well as the classroom student. Enrich your personal study or quiet time. Shorten your class or small-group preparation time as you gain valuable insights in the truths of God's Word that you can pass along to your students or group members.

DESIGNED FOR QUICK ACCESS

Those with time restraints will especially appreciate the timesaving features built into the *Shepherd's Notes*. All features are intended to aid a quick and concise encounter with the heart of the message.

Concise Commentary. The Acts narrative is replete with characters, places, and events. Short sections provide quick "snapshots" of the running narrative, highlighting important points and other information.

Outlined Text. A comprehensive outline covers the entire text of Acts. This is a valuable feature for following the narrative's flow, allowing for a quick, easy way to locate a particular passage.

Shepherd's Notes. These summary statements appear at the close of every key section of the narrative. While functioning in part as a quick summary, they also deliver the essence of the message presented in the sections which they cover.

Icons. Various icons in the margin highlight recurring themes in Acts and aid in selective searching or tracing of those themes.

Sidebars and Charts. These specially selected features provide additional background information to your study or preparation. These include definitions as well as cultural, historical, and biblical information.

Maps. These are placed at appropriate places in the book to aid your understanding and study of a text or passage.

Questions to Guide Your Study. These thought-provoking questions and discussion starters are designed to encourage interaction with the truth and principles of God's Word.

DESIGNED TO WORK FOR YOU

Personal Study. Using the *Shepherd's Notes* with a passage of Scripture can enlighten your study and take it to a new level. At your fingertips is information that would require searching several volumes to find. In addition, many points of application occur throughout the volume, contributing to personal growth.

Teaching. Outlines frame the text of Acts and provide a logical presentation of the message. Capsule thoughts designated as "Shepherd's Notes" provide summary statements for presenting the essence of key points and events. Application icons point out personal application of the message of Acts, and Historical Context and Cultural Context icons indicate where background information is supplied.

Group Study. *Shepherd's Notes* can be an excellent companion volume to use for gaining a quick but accurate understanding of the message of a Bible book. Each group member can benefit by having his or her own copy. The *Note's* format accommodates the study of or the tracing of themes throughout Acts. Leaders may use its flexible features to prepare for group sessions, or use them during group sessions.

"Questions to Guide Your Study" can spark discussion of the key points and truths of the message of Acts.

MARGIN ICONS USED IN ACTS

 Shepherd's Notes. Placed at the end of each section, a capsule statement that provides the reader with the essence of the message of that section.

 Old Testament Reference. Used when the writer refers to Old Testament Scripture passages that are related or have a bearing on the passage's understanding or interpretation.

 New Testament Reference. Used when the writer refers to New Testament passages that are related to or have a bearing on the passage's understanding or interpretation.

 Historical Background. To indicate historical, cultural, geographical, or biographical information that sheds light on the understanding or interpretation of a passage.

Personal Application. Used when the text provides a personal or universal application of truth.

Word Picture. Indicates that the meaning of a specific word or phrase is illustrated so as to shed light on it.

The Church happened. That is the fact of the matter. No human *person* set out to create the Church.

The basic purpose of the Book of Acts is to show the unimpeded spread of the Church throughout the Roman world. Underlying that obvious purpose is Luke's aim to show that this spread took place in the power of the Holy Spirit as the gospel penetrated geographical, social, racial, and religious barriers. This narrative is Luke's account of how the Holy Spirit worked through men and women to proclaim and live out the news of God's coming for all the peoples of the world.

AUTHOR

Luke is author of both the Book of Acts and the Gospel of Luke. He was a close friend and traveling companion of Paul. Many scholars believe that Luke wrote his Gospel and Acts in Rome with Paul during the apostle's first Roman imprisonment. Apparently Luke remained nearby or with Paul during that time, for Paul wrote in 2 Tim. 4:11, "Only Luke is with me."

Lukan authorship of Acts remained relatively unchallenged until critical approaches to the New Testament developed. In spite of some modern objections to Luke as the author of Acts, the ancient view of the early church still carries weight.

Acceptance of Luke as author of the Book of Acts was generally followed without serious question in the early church. Early Christian leaders such as Irenaeus, Clement of Alexandria, and Eusebius provide evidence for the Lukan authorship of Acts. The Muratorian Canon (A.D. 190) listed Luke as the author of Acts.

LUKE THE PERSON

Luke was probably a Gentile. Paul's reference to Luke in Col. 4:14 indicates that Luke was a physician. No other certain information about Luke's background exists. However, the

Anti-Marcionite prologue to Luke's Gospel, dating from the second century A.D., states that he was a native of Antioch, Syria, never married, and died in Boeotia at the age of eighty-four.

AUDIENCE

"Theophilus"

Some hold that his name is simply a generalization like "dear reader." Others prefer to think of him as a real person and as a pillar of some church. The name *Theophilus* means "loved by God."

From where did Luke write Acts, and to whom did he write? These questions probably are unanswerable. Luke dedicated his book to Theophilus, which is a Greek name. Did Luke write primarily to Gentiles? If so, why did he concern himself so much with Jewish questions? Why the elaborate messianic proofs of Peter's sermons in Acts 2 and 3 if not to provide his readers with a pattern for witness to the Jews? The most likely answer is that Luke intended his work for Christian communities that included both Jews and Gentiles—mixed congregations such as those we encounter frequently in Paul's Epistles.

PURPOSE

Luke's statement in the first two verses of Acts contrasts the purpose of the third Gospel, Luke, with the purpose of Acts. The Gospel of Luke was an account of what Jesus began to do and to teach up to the Ascension. Acts is an account of the continuation of Jesus' work through the Holy Spirit at work in the early church. Luke traced the gospel from its beginning in Jerusalem into the very center of power in the empire, the city of Rome.

DATE OF WRITING

The date for the writing of Acts is linked to the date for the writing of Luke. Both books have the same author, and Luke's Gospel is the first volume of a two-volume work. The date for Luke's Gospel is likely set in the early sixties. The most significant factor contributing to this date is the abrupt ending of Acts. The most cogent explanation of why Luke ended Acts with Paul still imprisoned is that Paul's imprisonment was still unresolved. The fact that Paul had spent two years (Acts 28:30) in a Roman prison at the conclusion of Acts provides help in dating Acts in the early sixties. At the conclusion of Acts, Paul was still awaiting trial. The Emperor Nero had not yet turned against the Christians as he did in A.D. 64. Therefore, Luke wrote Acts at some time in the early sixties.

STRUCTURE

Acts falls into two divisions: the mission of the Jerusalem church (chaps. 1–12) and the mission of Paul (chaps. 13–28). Each may be subdivided into two main sections. In the Jerusalem portion, chapters 1–5 treat the early church in Jerusalem, and chapters 6–12 treat the outreach beyond Jerusalem. In the Pauline portion, 13:1–21:16 relate the three major missions of Paul, and 21:27–28:31 deal with Paul's defense of his ministry.

LITERARY FORM

Acts is a history written with a purpose in view. Luke was not interested in outlining each facet of the development of the early church. Rather, he focused on how the gospel spread from Jerusalem to Rome. He also paid close attention to the work and ministry of Paul. Although Luke had a theological purpose for writing, we must understand that Acts contains reliable, trustworthy historical information.

BASIC OUTLINE OF ACTS

  I. Peter: Missionary to the Jews (1:1–12:24)
  A. The Early Church in Jerusalem (1:1–5:42)
  B. The Outreach beyond Jerusalem
     (6:1–12:24)

II. Paul: Missionary to the Gentiles
(12:25–28:31)

A. The Three Major Missions of Paul
(13:1–21:16)

B. Paul's Defense of His Ministry
(21:27–28:31)

ACTS 1

PROLOGUE (1:1–5)

Literary Prologue (vv. 1–2)

Clearly, the Book of Acts is a continuation of Luke's Gospel, which Luke refers to as his "former book." As with his Gospel, Luke writes this letter to Theophilus.

Luke provides an interesting summary of his Gospel and its relationship to Acts. His Gospel contained "all that Jesus began to do and to teach." This may imply that the work was unfinished. Indeed the work and words of Jesus continue throughout Acts in the ministry of the Apostles and other faithful witnesses. And that work still goes on in the work of the church today.

As with any good two-volume work, there is careful overlapping so that the reader can get his bearings. The connecting overlap between Luke and Acts is the Ascension of Jesus. Before Jesus went back to the Father, He gave commandments to His disciples (see Luke 24:44–49). The ministry of the Holy Spirit soon became a reality in the lives of the Apostles. The Holy Spirit would enable and empower them in their newly commissioned tasks.

Ten Major Sermons in Acts

REFERENCE IN ACTS	AUDIENCE	CENTRAL TRUTHS
Peter's Mission Sermons: 1. Acts 2:14-41	An international group of God-fearing Jews in Jerusalem for Pentecost	The gift of the Holy Spirit proves now is the age of salvation. Jesus' resurrection validates His role as Messiah.
2. Acts 3:11-26	A Jewish crowd in the Jerusalem Temple	The healing power of Jesus' name proves that He is alive and at work. Those who rejected the Messiah in ignorance can still repent.
3. Acts 10:27-48	The Gentile Cornelius and his household.	God accepts persons of all races who respond in faith to the gospel message.
Stephen's Sermon: 4. Acts 7:1-60	The Sanhedrin	God revealed Himself outside the Holy Land. God's people capped a history of rejecting the leaders He had sent them by killing the Messiah.
Paul's Mission Sermons: 5. Acts 13	Jews in the synagogue in Pisidian Antioch	Paul's mission sermons illustrate the changing focuses of the early Christian mission work: first Jewish evangelism, second Gentile evangelism, third development of Christian leaders.
6. Acts 17	Pagan Greeks at the Areopagus in Athens.	
7. Acts 20	Christian leaders of the Ephesian church	
Paul's Defense Sermons: 8. Acts 22:1-21	Temple crowd in Jerusalem	Paul's defense sermons emphasize that Paul was innocent of any breach of Roman law. Paul was on trial for his conviction that Jesus had been raised from the dead and had commissioned him as a missionary to the Gentiles.
9. Acts 24:10-21	The Roman Governor Felix	
10. Acts 26	The Jewish King Agrippa II	

A Short Chronology of Paul and Beyond

DATE	EVENT
Summer 44	Paul returned to Antioch
Spring 45	First missionary journey begun
Summer 47	First missionary journey ended
48	Jerusalem council
Summer 49	Second missionary journey begun
Spring 53	Paul before Gallio
Late fall 53	Second missionary journey ended
Spring 54	Third missionary journey begun
Late summer 54	Paul's arrival in Ephesus
Summer 57	Paul's departure from Ephesus
November 57	Paul's arrival in Corinth
February 58	Paul's departure from Corinth
Late April 58	Paul's departure from Philippi
Late summer 58	Paul's arrival in Jerusalem, third missionary journey ended, Paul arrested
Summer 60	Paul before Festus
Late summer 60	Paul sailed for Rome
Late October 60	Shipwrecked on Malta
Late January 61	Paul sailed for Italy
Early Spring 61	Paul arrived in Rome
63	Paul's imprisonment ended

Instructions Prior to Pentecost (vv. 3–5)

For forty of the most unusual days this earth has experienced, the risen Christ presented Himself alive. Hundreds, maybe thousands, had seen Jesus die. To refute His detractors—but even more, to undergird His disciples—the resurrected Jesus conducted a ministry of personal appearances.

He came to the disciples to give them courage to for their mission. By His words and visibility

Paul's Mission Travels and Letters

BOOK OF ACTS	ACTIVITY	APPROXIMATE DATE	WRITING
9:1–9	Paul's conversion	34–35	
9:26–29	Visit to Jerusalem	37–38	
11:27–30	Second visit to Jerusalem	48	
13–14	First Mission (Cyprus and Galatia)	48–50	Galatians
15	Jerusalem council	50	
16:1–18:22	Second mission (Galatia, Macedonia, Greece)	51–53	1, 2 Thessalonians
18:23–21:4	Third mission (Ephesus, Macedonia, Greece)	54–57	1, 2 Corinthians, Romans
21:15–26:32	Arrest in Jerusalem, trials and imprisonment in Caesarea	58–60	
27–28	Voyage to Rome, Roman imprisonment	60–63	Philemon, Colossians, Ephesians, Philippians
27–28	Release, further work, final imprisonment, and death	60–63	1 Timothy, Titus, 2 Timothy

Jesus assured them that the same God who had snatched Him from the clutches of death would be with them as they lived out their commission to go into all the world and make disciples of the nations.

■ *For forty days after the Resurrection, Jesus*
■ *appeared personally to the disciples on many*
■ *occasions. His instructions gave them cour-*
■ *age and assured them of His presence and*
■ *power in the days ahead.*

"Many Convincing Proofs"

During these forty days Jesus gave "many convincing proofs" that He was alive. The Greek word for "proofs" comes from logic and means demonstrative proof or evidence.

7

CHRIST'S LEGACY: THE CALL TO WITNESS (1:6–8)

The disciples asked Jesus about when the kingdom would be restored to Israel. Jesus turned aside their speculation. The "times and dates" of such things were matters within God's own purposes and authority. Instead, He directed the disciples toward their task which was to be His witnesses. Jesus promised them power for this world-sized task. Verse 8 provides a rough geographical scope of their mission: to "Jerusalem, and in all Judea and Samaria, and to the ends of the earth."

THE ASCENSION OF CHRIST (1:9–11)

The Ascension concluded Jesus' earthly ministry. It allowed eyewitnesses to see both the risen Christ on earth and victorious, and the eternal Christ returning to heaven to minister at the right hand of the Father.

Contrasted to Christ's act of humbling Himself to move from heaven to earth, and especially to the cross, is God's act of exalting Jesus.

■ *The Ascension of Jesus expanded Christ's*
■ *ministry from its geographically limited*
■ *earthly dimensions to its universal heavenly*
■ *dimensions. He now occupies the highest*
■ *position in the universe, in charge of every-*
■ *thing that exists and all that happens.*

PREPARATION IN THE UPPER ROOM (1:12–14)

The Disciples returned to Jerusalem from the Mount of Olives to wait as Jesus had commanded them. They gathered in an upper room of a large Palestinian house. Those present included the eleven disciples, "the women," including Mary the mother Jesus, and Jesus' brothers. Their primary activity was prayer. The time before Pentecost was a time of waiting, a time spent in prayer undoubtedly for the promised Spirit and for the power to witness.

RESTORATION OF THE APOSTOLIC CIRCLE (1:15–26)

During the period of prayer and waiting, an essential item of business was to restore the apostolic circle of the Twelve. Peter, clearly having become the leader of the group, addressed the assembly.

Judas's Defection (vv. 15–20)

Judas's defection from the ranks of the Twelve sparked the need to find a replacement. Peter referred to the Old Testament Scriptures for direction. He quoted Ps. 109:8 as a prophecy foretelling Jesus' betrayal by a friend. He also quoted from Ps. 69:25, which He saw as pointing to the desertion of Judas's place among the Apostles. He saw that psalm as already fulfilled.

Matthias's Installation (vv. 21–26)

The qualifications for Judas's replacement were: (1) he had to be a person who had witnessed Jesus' entire ministry, from His baptism by John to His ascension; and above all, (2) he had to have witnessed the Resurrection. The assembly put forward the names of two candidates: Joseph and Matthias. To select Judas's successor, they prayed for God's guidance and then cast lots. The lot fell to Matthias, and so he joined the eleven. Matthias, receives no further mention in Scripture.

"They all joined together"

This phrase (one word in the Greek language) is a favorite adverb of Luke's—"together." It is a word that means "with one mind." Luke uses it ten times in Acts. It expresses unity of purpose and particularly applies to the "one heart and mind" (4:32) of Christian fellowship (1:14; 2:1; 4:24; 5:12; 15:25).

"Let his life be cut short, and let another man replace him as leader.
Ps. 109:8 NCV

"May their place be empty; leave no one to live in their tents."
Ps. 65:25 NCV

Matthias means "gift of God."

■ *The assembly of Apostles chose a replace-*
■ *ment for Judas, betrayer of Jesus. After pray-*
■ *ing and casting lots, the group selected*
■ *Matthias as the new apostle.*

QUESTIONS TO GUIDE YOUR STUDY

1. What is the relationship between the book of Acts and the Gospel of Luke?

2. In what ways did the Ascension change Jesus' ministry?

3. The Disciples asked about when the kingdom of God would be realized. What did the restoration of the kingdom involve?

ACTS 2

Pentecost

Pentecost is one of the feasts of ancient Judaism that had its roots in Lev. 23:15–21. Through the years it was variously called the Feast of Weeks or the Feast of Firstfruits. And it was scheduled to begin at the close of harvesttime. It is called Pentecost because it began on the fiftieth day from the first Sunday after Passover.

The events in chapter 1 were a preparation for the outpouring of the Spirit on the praying band of believers during the Jewish festival known as Pentecost. In this chapter, their prayer was answered in a mighty way.

THE MIRACLE AT PENTECOST (2:1–13)

The miracle at Pentecost has been referred to as "the birth of the Church." A significant parallel between Pentecost and Luke's infancy narrative is the prominent role of the Spirit in both.

The Gift of the Holy Spirit (vv. 1–4)

Luke describes the coming of the Spirit in three carefully constructed parallel statements, each pointing to an aspect of the event.

The result of the Spirit's coming is that those in the upper room were "filled with the Holy Spirit." From this point on in Acts, the gift of the Spirit became a normal experience upon becoming a Christian. In this particular event,

- a sound came . . . and it filled the house (v. 2);
- tongues of fire appeared . . . and rested on each of them (v. 3);
- they began to speak in other tongues.

The event was audible and visible, and it manifested itself in an outward demonstration of inspired speech. The audible part is described as a rushing, mighty wind.

These events evoked Old Testament images. The violent wind and tongues of fire were familiar signs of the presence of God, especially connected with Mount Sinai. The miracle of communication in many languages reversed the curse of Babel.

The Witness to the Spirit (vv. 5–13)

Gathered were "God-fearing Jews from every nation under heaven." Likely these were Diaspora Jews who had returned from other nations to Jerusalem to live. Luke lists the names of the various nationalities present. It encompassed the Roman world, spanning what is present-day Iran, the Middle East, Turkey, North Africa, and west to Rome.

The crowd responded in two different ways to the "wonders" of God they had just seen. Some made fun of them, while others were amazed and asked, "What does this mean?"

God gave the church the gift of the Holy Spirit. The Spirit's arrival was audible, visible, and manifested itself in an outward demonstration of inspired speech. The event of Pentecost meant that the gospel was now able to reach the world through the power of the Spirit.

Ability to Speak in Different Languages

At Pentecost, the church received the gift to communicate the gospel in foreign languages (Acts 2; cp. 10:44–46; 19:6). The Apostles spoke in foreign languages they had not previously studied. Jews from every Diaspora nation were amazed that the Galileans were able to speak in their languages. God gave His Spirit to all His people to witness and prophesy.

PETER'S SERMON AT PENTECOST (2:14–41)

Peter's sermon is the first of many sermons and speeches in Acts. Luke recorded both the content and tone of these sermons. Peter's sermon is the heart of this chapter. The controversial and exciting nature of the pentecostal experience had attracted significant attention. The true focus of the chapter, however, is the beginning of Christian evangelism.

Two Themes Run through the Sermon

Peter's primary theme is that Jesus' life, death, and resurrection happened according to God's plan. A second theme is the Jewish responsibility for Jesus' death.

The sermon evoked a response in the form of a question: "Brothers, what shall we do?" Peter's answer was an offer to repent and be baptized. The response to Peter's invitation was overwhelming. About three thousand people "accepted his message" and were baptized.

■ *Peter delivered the first Christian apology*
■ *(defense) in the history of the Church on the*
■ *day of Pentecost. His address expanded on*
■ *two simple themes: repentance and baptism*
■ *are to be done in the name of Jesus Christ.*

THE FLAVOR OF THE FIRST NEW COMMUNITY (2:42–47)

This first picture provides a snapshot of the Church immediately after its beginnings. The picture is one of maturing discipleship. The new converts were being taught, they continued to worship in the temple, and they were unified economically and spiritually. Finally, God was continuing to add "to their number daily." The Church was not only surviving, but it was also growing.

QUESTIONS TO GUIDE YOUR STUDY

1. What events took place at Pentecost? Describe the significance of each.
2. What two themes ran through Peter's sermon at Pentecost?
3. In his narrative, Luke provides several summaries about the progress of the church. How might your church's growth parallel that of the early church?

ACTS 3

THE FIRST RECORDED HEALING (3:1–10)

Peter and John were going up to the temple at the time of prayer. When they arrived at one of the temple's gates, a "lame man" was in the process of being carried and placed there to beg for alms from those entering the temple. The man is described as crippled from birth. Those who entered the temple for the evening sacrifice and prayer would be particularly disposed to practice their piety by generously giving alms to a lame beggar. Almsgiving was one of the main ways to show kindness, and thus was considered a major expression of a person's devotion to God.

Almsgiving

Although the Hebrew language had no technical term to refer to "alms" or "almsgiving," the practice of charitable giving especially to the poor, became a very important belief and practice within Judaism.

When Peter and John encountered the lame man, Peter told the man to look at them. They did in the name of Jesus what Jesus Himself had done so many times. Peter said to the lame man,

Of the many miracles recounted in Acts, none has more formal resemblance to the miracles of Jesus in the Gospels than this one. There is one major difference—Jesus healed by His own authority, whereas Peter healed by the "name" of Jesus, which was indeed by Jesus' authority at work through the agency of the Apostles.

"Silver or gold I do not have, but what I have I give to you. In the name of Jesus Christ of Nazareth, walk" (v. 6). Instantly, the man's feet and ankles became strong. He jumped, walked, and leaped, calling attention to himself as he accompanied Peter and John into the temple courts. Verse 6 is the heart of the message, the one detail that sets this story apart from the usual narrative. Some things are more precious than silver or gold.

Those who were unworthy for worship in the old religion of Israel found full acceptance in the name of Jesus. The healing of the lame man amazed those who witnessed it and prepared them for Peter's explanation.

PETER'S SERMON IN THE TEMPLE (3:11–26)

The scene of Peter's next speech was Solomon's Colonnade, probably a covered area located on the eastern side of the temple, within the temple walls. As in the case of Pentecost, an apostolic action raised questions that gave Peter an opportunity to preach.

A comparison of this sermon and Peter's Pentecost sermon reveals that it is remarkably like his first sermon in both organization and content. Peter noted the will of God in the life, death, and resurrection of Jesus. He also emphasized the power of God to raise Jesus and gave a softer treatment of the Jewish responsibility for Jesus' death.

The two sermons contain significant differences as well. For example, the scriptural proofs in the

Pentecost sermon aim at establishing the messianic status of Jesus. Those in this sermon are aimed at the need for the Jews to repent and accept Jesus as the one sent from God.

Peter gave the threefold result of repentance: (1) their sins would be forgiven, (2) the "times of refreshing" would come upon them, and (3) God would send the Messiah whom He had appointed for them.

Peter quoted Moses as one of the earliest Hebrew prophets to announce the coming of Messiah:

"The Lord your God will raise up for you a prophet like me from among you, from your countrymen, you shall listen to him."
Deut. 18:15 NASB

Peter delivered a stirring speech at the temple. He noted the will of God in the life, death, and resurrection of Jesus. He included scriptural proofs in his sermon aimed at the need for the Jews to repent and accept Jesus as the one sent from God.

QUESTIONS TO GUIDE YOUR STUDY

1. By whose authority and power did Peter heal the lame man at the temple?
2. Why was almsgiving so important to the Jews? Do we have any modern-day counterparts to that practice?
3. What were the key points of Peter's sermon at the temple?

ACTS 4

To this point in Acts, there had been no resistance to the Christians on the part of the Jewish leaders. In fact, the picture had been that of general acceptance and favor accorded the early believers by the people. It was the officials, however, who turned against them. The primary enemy was the priestly Sadducean aristocracy for whom the Christians were a serious threat to the status quo.

THE FIRST ARREST (4:1–31)

The Arrest and Interrogation (vv. 1–12)

Peter's sermon at the temple was suddenly interrupted by an official group of priests, the captain of the temple guard, and Sadducees.

The Sadducees likely feared reaction from the governing Roman rulers. Peter and John were arrested and placed in jail overnight.

The two were then ordered to appear before the Sanhedrin and account for their actions. They were probably in as much trouble for Peter's message in the Temple as they were for healing the lame man. The question from the Sanhedrin was, "By what power or what name did you do this?"

Peter answered them through the power of the Spirit. His testimony was, in many ways, a condensed form of his address at the temple. Peter explained that the power by which the lame man was healed was that of Jesus of Nazareth. Not only that, but Peter accused the Sanhedrin of responsibility for rejecting and killing Christ. He also proclaimed God's power in raising Jesus from the dead.

Warning and Release (vv. 13–22)

In contrast to the Apostles' boldness and freedom, the Council sat in stony silence. After asking the Apostles to leave the courtroom, the Council assessed the evidence. It was hardly a clear-cut case. The Council's response was a political one. Although they were unable to deny the apostolic miracle, they felt compelled to curtail the apostolic preaching. Peter and

The Sanhedrin

The Sanhedrin was the highest Jewish council in the first century. The word Sanhedrin is usually translated "council" in English versions of the Bible. The Council had seventy-one members over which a high priest presided. The Sanhedrin included both of the main Jewish parties among its membership. Since the high priest presided, the Sadducean priestly party seems to have been predominant, but some leading Pharisees also were members.

John were warned to no longer speak "in this name." The Council had no alternative but to threaten the Apostles and then release them.

The Prayer of the Community (vv. 23–31)

These verses give us a glimpse into the life of the Christians in Jerusalem. It is a report of the church's prayer of gratitude for God's deliverance of the Apostles from the Jewish authorities. In response to their prayer for power and strength, their meeting place was shaken with the presence of the Spirit.

- *Through the power of His Spirit, God delivered the Apostles from the Jewish authorities.*
- *God's Spirit shook the meeting place of the Christians who had gathered to pray for the Apostles. The result of the Spirit's presence was a renewed boldness by the church in proclaiming the gospel.*

THE COMMON LIFE OF THE COMMUNITY (4:32–37)

This second summary amplifies one of the ideas introduced in the first: their common possessions. The Christians were living in harmony and unity. The proof of their unity was their willingness to share resources with one another. Through the charity of wealthier members, like Barnabas, those who were poor received enough. As a result, no one among them was "needy" (4:34).

Barnabas

Barnabas means son of encouragement. This is the name given to Joseph, a Levite from Cyprus.

QUESTIONS TO GUIDE YOUR STUDY

1. How was the early church initially received by the Jewish authorities?

2. What annoyed and angered the Sanhedrin about Peter and John's preaching?

3. The early church was a praying church. How did they pray? What might we learn from their example?

ACTS 5

Church

The word for "church" (Greek word *ekklesia*) is first used in Acts 5:11. It meant a free assembly of people. The Christian Church was old and new: new in that it gave testimony to the life, death, resurrection, and ongoing ministry of Jesus; and old because the idea of the assembly reached back to the people of God created in the Exodus.

ANANIAS AND SAPPHIRA (5:1–11)

Like Barnabas, Ananias and Sapphira sold property and gave the proceeds to the church. Unlike Barnabas, they agreed to lie about their profit from the sale. No doubt they were glad to be part of the movement and were serious about their involvement. Ananias and Sapphira were not as secure as Barnabas. Whereas Barnabas could freely and with no strings attached give his money to the church and brush aside the flattery, Ananias and his wife craved the adulation but could not quite bring themselves to part with all their goods. They would go after the best of both worlds: sell the property and make a show of giving it to the church, but keep part of the proceeds hidden.

Peter saw through the attempt. He questioned the man, "Ananias, how is it that Satan has so filled your heart that you have lied to the Holy Spirit and have kept back for yourself some of the money you received for the land?"

Ananias had violated his own integrity, perjured the very Spirit of God who now lived in his life, and made a mockery of the Holy Spirit's activity in his soul. Peter declared to Ananias, "You have not lied to men but to God." With that, he fell down and died.

Three hours later Sapphira arrived. When the Apostle confronted her with the joint sin, she too fell dead. The same people who buried Ananias prepared her body for burial and placed her beside her husband.

This event had a powerful effect on the church. God's quick and decisive punishment created great fear in the church. Its members were terrified—a natural response to witnessing the power of God. This event has little to do with the amount a person gives. The importance lies with one's attitude. Ananias and Sapphira gave their offering to impress the congregation. The fact that they held back money and claimed they had given the entire sale price reflected a self-serving attitude, not one that served God.

 Such immediate and radical judgment is not the usual way God deals with believers today. However, judgment, punishment for sin, and retribution are part of God's way of running a balanced moral universe. We need to get the message that we do not go on sinning with impunity, thinking that we won't have to reckon with God and others for our misdeeds.

ℜ

- *Ananias and Sapphira, like Barnabas, sold*
- *some property and gave the proceeds to the*
- *church. They held back some of the proceeds*
- *but asserted that they had given the entire*
- *sale price. God's judgment was immediate*
- *death. The sin of Ananias and Sapphira was*
- *not that they kept some of the profit. Their*
- *sin was in lying to God and to the Apostles by*
- *misrepresenting their act of giving.*

Apostolic Preaching

In their public preaching, the Apostles directed their message to the unconverted. They stressed the gospel of Christ and preached for conversions. The Apostles' message had several essential elements in common:

1. They proclaimed that Scripture had been fulfilled.

2. The fulfillment came in the person of Jesus, whom they claimed as Messiah.

3. Salvation comes through the death, burial, and resurrection of Jesus, who has ascended to the right hand of God from where He will come again to judge the world.

4. Salvation consists in the forgiveness of sins and the gift of the Holy Spirit. When sin is taken away, and the Holy Spirit comes in, a person has received eternal life.

5. The appropriate response to this gospel is repentance toward God and faith in the Lord Jesus.

Luke's second summary and story of Ananias and Sapphira provided an interlude within the larger story of the conflict between the Apostles and the Jewish authorities.

THE MIRACLES WORKED BY THE APOSTLES (5:12–16)

This is the third summary statement in Acts. It emphasizes the healing ministry of the Apostles and bears out the divine response to their prayer for signs and wonders. This passage, with its focus on the healing ministry and growing acclaim of the people, prepared for the renewed concern of the Sadducees and their arrest of the Apostles.

THE APOSTLES BEFORE THE COUNCIL (5:17–42)

In the previous section (3:1–4:31), the Sanhedrin had instructed the Apostles not to teach and preach the gospel. With the growing success of the Christian witness came a heightened reaction on the part of the Jewish authorities. As before, the Sadducees were enraged by the Apostles' preaching.

Arrest, Escape, and Rearrest (vv. 17–26)

An angel of the Lord appeared to the imprisoned Apostles at night, opened the prison doors, and led them out. The angel then gave them God's instructions. They were to return to the temple and speak "the full message of this new life." That is, they were to resume their witness and preach the message of salvation.

The Second Appearance before the Sanhedrin (vv. 27–40)

Whereas the first meeting with the Sanhedrin involved only Peter and John, in this second appearance, all the Apostles stood before the Council.

Interestingly, the high priest made no reference to the Apostles' escape, perhaps out of embarrassment. However, formal charges were brought this time. The Apostles had been duly warned by the court to no longer continue their witness, and they had ignored the warning. They were accused not only of speaking and preaching, but also of disobeying the Sanhedrin's specific order.

In response, the Apostles echoed Acts 4:19: "We must obey God rather than men!" Again Peter accused the Jews of murdering Jesus, and then he proclaimed Jesus' resurrection. Peter's words were met with murderous anger. Some members of the Council even called for the death penalty.

At this point Gamaliel, identified as a Pharisee, intervened. He was the voice of moderation. He urged the Sanhedrin to spare the Apostles, appealing to the history of other messianic movements. Persuaded by Gamaliel's speech, the Sanhedrin decided to spare the Apostles.

Release and Witness (vv. 41–42)
Again, the Apostles were released, but this time with a flogging. Likely, each received thirty-nine lashes. The flogging was a warning not to persist in their offense.

The Apostles, however, were not persuaded. They would continue to obey God rather than men.

Gamaliel

Gamaliel was a highly regarded Pharisee who was a member of the Sanhedrin. He squelched a plan by the Sanhedrin to kill the Apostles by reminding the members that interference with what the Apostles were doing might prove to be opposition to God. If the work of the Apostles was a purely human work, Gamaliel said, it would come to nothing anyway. According to Acts 22:3, this Gamaliel had been Paul's teacher. He was the grandson of the great Rabbi Hillel. He died about A.D 52.

- *The Apostles were brought before the Sanhe-*
- *drin for a second time because of their wit-*
- *ness for Christ. Although their lives were*
- *spared, they were flogged for their "offense."*
- *Undaunted by their punishment, the Apostles*
- *continued to preach and worship, praising*
- *God for being able to suffer for the name of*
- *Christ.*

END OF THE FIRST SECTION OF ACTS

This ends the first major section of Acts. Luke's two major themes have been skillfully interwoven throughout these narratives. The gospel, through God's power, had overcome the barriers of language and persecution. The Spirit had been poured out on the church, empowering it to minister and grow. The Christian church has been portrayed as a group of devout Jews who wanted nothing more than to be able to worship and minister without obstruction. The Jewish authorities, however, were unwilling to allow free reign to those who confessed Jesus as Messiah. And so, a process of separation begins within Judaism. Out of this separation, the Church will emerge.

QUESTIONS TO GUIDE YOUR STUDY

1. What was the sin of Ananias and Sapphira? Why was God so decisive in His punishment?
2. What were the elements of apostolic preaching?
3. What was the attitude of the Apostles at their second appearance before the Sanhedrin? What were the results of their trial?

ACTS 6

The church now faces a problem and finds a way of solving it.

APPOINTMENT OF THE SEVEN (6:1–7)

The Problem (v. 1–2)

For the first time a major division confronted the church. Conflicts had arisen between the Hellenists (Grecian Jews) and Hebraists (Aramaic-speaking Jews). The conflict came to a head because a large number of Hellenistic widows needed assistance. One of the ministries of the synagogue (and the church) was to provide food and assistance to those widows and children not supported by relatives. Perhaps most of the widows who needed help were Hellenistic widows, and a conflict arose over the proper distribution of food.

The Solution (vv. 3–4)

The Apostles proposed a solution that pleased the entire community. That solution involved selecting a group of men to administer this assistance to widows. Like the Apostles, these men were chosen for their wisdom and their spirituality.

Selection and Installation (vv. 5–6)

The church selected their ministers and set the Seven apart for their ministry. Stephen is named first, and he becames the primary character in the following narrative. He is followed by Philip, who would become a major figure in the expanding Christian witness. The other five—Procorus, Nicanor, Timon, Parmenas, and Nicolas from Antioch—play no further role in Acts.

The church presented these men to the Apostles, who confirmed the church's decision by praying and laying hands on the Seven.

Hellenists

Those whose language and culture was Greek, even though they may not have been Greek by race. The word is derived from *hellas*, which is the Greek word for *Greece*.

Stephen

Stephen became the first Christian martyr. He was the central member of the Seven chosen to bring peace to the quarreling church (Acts 6:1–7). He was so mighty in the Scriptures that his Jewish opponents could not refute him as he argued that Jesus was the Messiah (Acts 6:10). Saul of Tarsus heard Stephen's speech to the Jewish Sanhedrin, which accused the Jewish leaders of rejecting God's way as had their forefathers. Saul held the clothes of those who stoned Stephen to death, but saw Stephen die a victorious death. Stephen may have been the human agency that God used to conquer Saul, who became the great Christian missionary.

■ *Conflict within the community was resolved*
■ *by choosing seven men who would adminis-*
■ *ter the church's welfare system. By selecting*
■ *the Seven, the Apostles were free to carry out*
■ *their primary responsibilities of preaching*
■ *and bearing witness to Christ.*

Transition (v. 7)

The narrative about Stephen is a major turning point in Acts. It ends a series of three trials before the Sanhedrin. The Stephen episode is the culmination in the witness to the Jews of Jerusalem.

STEPHEN'S ARREST (6:8–12)

Stephen's role in Acts is foreshadowed by the way Luke introduces him in 6:5, "a man full of faith and of the Holy Spirit." Stephen had been acting more like an apostle than a deacon. He had been doing miracles, and none of the Hellenistic Jews could win an argument with him.

Stephen's Debate with the Hellenist Synagogue (vv. 8–10)

Members from the Synagogue of the Freedmen were disturbed by Stephen's preaching and ministry. (Their name *Freedmen* may have referred to their identity as former slaves or descendants of captives taken from Palestine during the Diaspora.)

The Frame-Up (vv. 11–12)

Unable to resist Stephen's persuasive power and his logic, the Hellenist Jews resorted to underhanded methods. Their plan to stop Stephen included conspiracy, perjury, and mob psychology. They charged Stephen with blasphemy against the temple and the Law. They then seized him and brought him before the Sanhedrin.

THE TRIAL BEGINS (6:13–7:1)

The trial provided a forum for Stephen to speak with passion and persuasion in the triumph of the Spirit. Before he spoke, Luke reminded us of his power. As the charges were brought against him, all attention turned to Stephen to see how he would respond. His face looked like that of an angel, a true sign of God's presence.

As the trial began, the high priest asked Stephen, "Are these charges true?" In our present-day court system that question would translate into, "How do you plead, guilty or innocent?"

■ *Disturbed at Stephen's preaching and teach-*
■ *ing, Hellenist Jews charged Stephen with*
■ *blasphemy against the temple and the Law.*
■ *He was arrested and brought before the San-*
■ *hedrin.*

QUESTIONS TO GUIDE YOUR STUDY

1. Describe the division that confronted the new church. What solution was reached?
2. Why were the Hellenist Jews at odds with Stephen?
3. What was Stephen's role in the growth of the early church?

Acts 7

STEPHEN'S SPEECH BEFORE THE SANHEDRIN (7:2–53)

Overview

Stephen expressed three main ideas in his speech. The first was the Jewish reverence for the Holy Land. Most Jews were convinced that the land was God's greatest gift to them, and they considered Palestine to be the place where God lived and worked.

Heaven is My Throne, And earth is the footstool of My feet; What kind of house will you build for Me, says the Lord; or what place is there for My repose? Was it not My hand which made all these things?"
Isa. 66:1

Second, Stephen showed that Moses, the one venerated by the Jews as the great giver of the Law, had been constantly disobeyed by the Jews. Finally, Stephen noted that God allowed Solomon to build the temple because the Jews demanded it. God Himself was satisfied with the nomadic life of the tabernacle.

Stephen began his speech with great deference to his hearers, reminding them they were his fellow Jewish "brothers," and he showed respect to the elders of the Sanhedrin by referring to them as "fathers."

Stephen denied that God was tied to any land, recounting the history of the patriarchs and showing that God worked in their lives much more outside the promised land than within. It was to a "landless" Abraham that God gave the promises to Israel.

Stephen's speech climaxed in strong words toward the Jewish leaders. He termed them "stiff-necked" and accused them of denying God's prophets, Spirit, and Messiah. In response to the charge of blasphemy against the temple, Stephen accused the Jews of failing to obey the Law of which they were so proud.

■ *Stephen's speech is important in understand-*
■ *ing the way in which the gospel moved from*
■ *its Jewish beginnings to a Gentile world.*
■ *That the Jews rejected the gospel should be*
■ *no surprise. Stephen asserted that they had*
■ *rejected the will of God throughout their his-*
■ *tory as God's chosen people.*

STEPHEN'S MARTYRDOM (7:54–8:1*a*)

Whether Stephen intended to give a direct appeal for his hearers to repent, we will never know, for they abruptly broke him off. They were livid at his placing them on trial. Luke described their rage as "cut to the heart." Swiftly, before the Roman soldiers could be alerted, Stephen was dragged, kicked, and tossed outside the city gates, thrown into the stoning pit, and quickly bludgeoned to death.

In his final gasps, pain was supplanted by God's gift of vision. Stephen declared, "I see heaven open and the Son of Man standing at the right hand of God." Jesus had spoken similar words at His appearance before the Sanhedrin. The vision confirmed Stephen's testimony. One can understand the furious response in the Sanhedrin at Stephen's testimony to his vision. They stood condemned by his words.

His last words, "Lord Jesus, receive my spirit," echoed those which Jesus prayed from the cross. Stephen died not in fear and despair but in victory.

Those who executed Stephen may have justified their action by reference to Lev. 24:14:
"Bring the one who has cursed outside the camp, and let all who heard him lay their hands on his head; then let all the congregation stone him."

■ *Stephen's death was not the end. To the con-*
■ *trary, his death was another phase in the*
■ *beginning of a new community that God was*
■ *bringing into existence.*

QUESTIONS TO GUIDE YOUR STUDY

1. What key points did Stephen drive home in his speech before the Sanhedrin?
2. What did Stephen say to the Sanhedrin that so angered them? What part did they play in Stephen's death?
3. What happened in the wake of Stephen's death?

ACTS 8

ENTER: SAUL OF TARSUS (8:1*a*)

It was no accident that young Saul of Tarsus witnessed the death of Stephen. He got frantically busy, trying to shake off the experience. Unable or unwilling to admit his feelings, he vented all his fears and frustrations on the believers. With the fury of a summer storm, he burst on the church, determined to stamp out this insidious movement. But all he succeeded in doing was furthering the spread of the gospel.

THE GOSPEL IN SAMARIA (8:1*b*)

Fleeing Jerusalem, new converts went to the outer region of Judea and even into Samaria.

It is of lasting credit to the early Christians that they pushed through their prejudices not only to live with the Samaritans, but to present them with the gospel.

STEPHEN IS BURIED (8:2)

The regulations of the Jews permitted burial for a criminal who had been stoned to death but prohibited any lamentation over him. Stephen's friends, however, disobeyed the rules and buried him with much lamentation and mourning.

THE LION OF GOD (8:3)

Venting his anger, Saul went tearing through the city and its environs, seeking converts, disrupting worship services, and hauling men and women off to prison. Such "holy" crusades quickly lose all bounds of reason. Saul's vendetta was no different. Although Luke's account is sparse, the picture is one of midnight raids, good people poorly treated, and human rights disregarded in the name of religion—for the sake of God.

UNDAUNTED PREACHERS (8:4)

In the face of the persecution following Stephen's death, the Christians were scattered. Ripped from homes and families, hounded out of town, fleeing under cover of darkness, followers of the Way ran in every direction. But they remained undaunted, counting themselves blessed to be able to suffer persecution for their Lord. As they spread throughout the area, they also spread the gospel.

Following Stephen's death, Saul, the persecutor of Christians, tore through the city of Jerusalem to carry on his vendetta. In the face of this persecution, the Christians were

"Saul the Persecutor"

Paul's Jewish name was Saul, given at birth after his father or some near kinsman, or even after the famous Old Testament King Saul, who like Paul was from the tribe of Benjamin. Being born in a Roman city and claiming Roman citizenship, Paul was his official Roman name. Tarsus, the place of Paul's birth (Acts 22:3), is still a bustling city a few miles from the Mediterranean Sea on Turkey's southern shore.

Paul eventually went to Jerusalem to study under the famous rabbi, Gamaliel. At that time, he was probably thirteen to eighteen years old. Paul became very zealous for the traditions and teachings of his people (Gal. 1:14). He was a Pharisee (Phil. 3:5). This zealous commitment to the study of the Old Testament laws and traditions is the background of Paul's persecution of his Jewish brothers who believed Jesus was the Messiah. Stephen's sermon before the Sanhedrin apparently stimulated Paul's persecution of the church.

Philip

Philip was a respected member of the church at Jerusalem who was chosen as one of the Seven—the first "deacons" (Acts 6:5). Following Stephen's martyrdom, Philip took the gospel to Samaria, where his ministry was blessed. Subsequently, he was led south to the Jerusalem-Gaza road, where he introduced the Ethiopian eunuch to Christ and baptized him (Acts 8:26–38). He was then transported by the Spirit to Azotus (Ashdod), and from there conducted an itinerant ministry until he took up residence in Caesarea. Then, for twenty years, we lose sight of him. He is last seen in Scripture when Paul lodged in his home on his journey to Jerusalem (Acts 21:8). He had four unmarried daughters who were prophetesses.

■ scattered. *As they spread throughout the*
■ *area, they also spread the gospel.*

PHILIP INVESTIGATES (8:5–8)

Philip, one of the Seven, found his way into Samaria. As with Stephen, the power of the Spirit was present in Philip's work. He preached and performed signs and wonders, such as healing and exorcising unclean spirits.

SIMON THE MAGICIAN BELIEVES (8:9–13)

Simon the Magician (sometimes called Simon Magus) stands in contrast to Philip and his works. Magic was a significant form of religious expression in the ancient world. As a result of Philip's ministry, many Samaritans came to faith, including Simon.

PETER INVESTIGATES SAMARIA AND MEETS SIMON (8:14–25)

No one had told the Samaritans about the Spirit. That dimension of Christian experience was missing from the group. But when Peter, who had experienced the Spirit, informed them of the grand possibility, they eagerly opened the windows of their souls to receive God's gift of the Holy Spirit.

Simon the Magician could not believe his eyes. When Peter prayed and laid hands on people, they received the Holy Spirit. Simon thought that if he could have that power, his act would be a real winner. His shallow commitment to Christ became abundantly clear. He saw the invoking of the Spirit as a way to enhance his magic show. He had the audacity to offer to buy the gift from Peter.

Peter informed the startled charlatan that he had never really had an experience with Jesus and that he would never receive the Spirit with this attitude. Peter answered him with, "Repent of this wickedness and pray to the Lord. Perhaps he will forgive you for having such a thought in your heart. For I see that you are full of bitterness and captive to sin."

Terrified, Simon begged Peter to pray that no ill consequences would fall on him.

THE WITNESS TO THE ETHIOPIAN TREASURER (8:26–40)

Philip's evangelistic activity did not end with Samaria. He was also chosen to participate in an advance of the gospel beyond Jerusalem, Judea, and Samaria. In response to the prompting of an angel, Philip went to a certain road in the desert and met an Ethiopian traveling home from a visit to Jerusalem. Philip was offered the opportunity to explain Scripture to the Ethiopian, to witness to him about Jesus, and to baptize him before being transported to another region by the power of the Spirit.

The conversion of the Ethiopian is placed in Luke's account between Philip's work in Samaria (in which one racial barrier is overcome) and the conversion of Cornelius in Acts 10. From a literary standpoint, we would assume that these stories serve as steps in the gospel's transition from Jews to Gentiles.

Simon

Luke does not mention Simon again, but the magician earned his negative place in history by giving his name to the practice of buying or selling a church office (simony).

■ *The Spirit, having broken down the racial*
■ *barrier that denied Samaritans religious*
■ *access to God, now breaks down a physical*
■ *barrier to faith as well. None would be*

- *judged based on racial or physical character-*
- *istics. Entry into the kingdom would depend*
- *solely on spiritual relationship with God.*

QUESTIONS TO GUIDE YOUR STUDY

1. How do you think Saul's experience of watching Stephen being stoned to death affected him?
2. What was the result of Saul's persecution which scattered the Christians to other communities?
3. What landmark truth did the conversion of the Ethiopian treasurer convey?

ACTS 9

GOD CALLS SAUL (9:1–30)

The first half of Saul's conversion account divides into three main sections: the appearance on the Damascus road (vv. 1–9), the ministry of Ananias to Saul (vv. 10–18a), and the final confirmation of Saul's conversion through his bold witness in the Jewish synagogues of Damascus (vv. 18b–22).

The Appearance on the Damascus Road (vv. 1–9)

As Saul approached the gates of Damascus, suddenly a great light from heaven flashed around him. The light must have been intense, for the time of the occurrence was "around midday." At the sight, Saul fell to the ground—a reaction found in the Old Testament from those who experienced a similar divine visitation. Then a voice came from heaven, "Saul, Saul, why do you persecute me?"

Saul answered, "Who are you, Lord?"

Damascus

Capital of Syria with close historical ties to Israel. It would have taken Saul at least six days to travel from Jerusalem to Damascus. This shows how far the Way had spread and how strongly Saul was motivated to stomp it out.

The response from heaven was: "I am Jesus, whom you are persecuting." Now Saul beheld Jesus and the undeniable proof that He both lived and reigned in glory. Saul was completely broken. The raging persecutor was brought to his knees. For three days he remained blinded and neither ate nor drank.

The Ministry of Ananias to Saul (vv. 10–18a)

In Damascus lived a disciple named Ananias. The Lord appeared to Ananias in a vision with instructions to seek out Saul at the house of Judas. At first, Ananias protested the commission. He knew who Saul was and was afraid of him. But Ananias obeyed and went to Saul, laying hands upon him so he might recover his sight. Ananias acted as God's agent in healing and baptizing Saul.

The scene in Judas's house concluded with Saul's receiving nourishment and recovering his strength.

Saul's Bold Witness in Damascus (vv. 18b–22)

Immediately Saul began to preach in the synagogues, serving the gospel with all the zeal he had formerly used to persecute it. He proclaimed Jesus as the "Son of God." Naturally, all who heard him were amazed that this noted enemy of the Way was now preaching Christ. Paul developed rapidly, and "grew more and more powerful." He soon became more than a match for the Jews with whom he debated.

Saul the Persecuted (vv. 23–31)

Saul was so successful in his witness that the Jews in Damascus plotted to kill him. This forced him to escape over the city wall and go to Jerusalem. The believers in Jerusalem were still afraid of him until Barnabas, acting as an

Saul's Conversion

With the conversion of Saul to the Christian faith, we have one of the most significant and far-reaching events in the history of the early church. There are three detailed accounts of this remarkable experience given in the New Testament. Luke records it here as historical fact, and Paul gives two accounts in his own words (Acts 22:6–11; 26:12–19).

encourager, vouched for Saul's sincerity and effectiveness in Damascus.

In a dramatic conversion experience, God called Saul to be His witness. Full of energy and zeal, Saul immediately began to preach and proclaim Jesus as the Son of God. The result of Saul's conversion was Christianity's most bitter enemy becoming its most ardent supporter.

PETER PERFORMS MIRACLES (9:32–43)

With Saul home in Tarsus, the narrative focuses once more on Peter. He last appeared in connection with the Samaritan mission (8:14–25). Now he participates in the greater Judean mission, evangelizing the coastal cities.

The Healing of Aeneas (vv. 32–35)

Lydda

During the NT era, it was the district capital of Samaria. Christianity became a strong influence in Lydda by the second century.

Peter stopped at Lydda to visit the believers there. He found a paralytic by the name of Aeneas, who had been bedridden for eight years. Peter took the initiative to heal Aeneas without any request, much as Jesus did on occasion. This healing was accomplished by a healing word, calling on the name of Jesus.

The Raising of Dorcas (vv. 36–43)

Joppa was the main port city of Judea, located on the Philistine coast. Here lived a female disciple named Tabitha. In his narrative, Luke provides the translation "Dorcas" for his Greek readers. Tabitha had become sick and died. Knowing that Peter was close by—a distance of three hours journey by foot—the Christians at Joppa sent two men to Lydda to urge Peter to hasten to Joppa without delay.

When Peter arrived, he was taken to the upper room where Tabitha had been placed. After dismissing the mourners, Peter knelt by her bed, fully aware that healing would not come from him, but only through him in the power of Christ. After praying, Peter ordered her to open her eyes. She did so and immediately got up from her bier. There was much rejoicing and no little fear and awe when the crowd saw Tabitha walk out with Peter. More people believed in Jesus and attached themselves to local communities of faith because of this mighty act of God.

■ *Peter participated in the greater Judean mis-*
■ *sion, evangelizing the coastal cities. Luke*
■ *records two key events from this mission: the*
■ *healing of the paralytic and the raising of Dor-*
■ *cas from the dead.*

QUESTIONS TO GUIDE YOUR STUDY

1. Saul had a dramatic conversion experience. What is especially striking to you about it?
2. Describe Ananias's feelings about helping Saul the persecutor. What might we learn from Ananias's response?
3. God turned Christianity's most bitter enemy into its most ardent supporter. What is your evaluation of the impact of this event on church members?

. . . .

Chapter 10 marks a high point in the church's expanding mission. God led Peter to witness to the Gentile Cornelius. Through that experience Peter became fully convinced of God's purpose to reach all peoples and hence became one of the greatest advocates of the mission to the Gentiles.

CORNELIUS THE CENTURION (10:1–2)

This section begins by introducing its first main character. His name was Cornelius, a centurion of the Italian Regiment who resided in Caesarea. Each detail of that statement is significant. That he was mentioned by name is perhaps indicative that he was well known in the early Christian communities for which Luke wrote. He was a military man with the rank of centurion, which placed him in command of one hundred soldiers.

CORNELIUS'S VISION (10:3–8)

Cornelius had a vision in which an angel from God appeared to him. His initial terror was eased when the angel called him by name and assured Cornelius that he had found favor with God because of his prayers and generosity to others. The angel instructed Cornelius to send a message to Joppa, to the house of Simon, a tanner, requesting Simon Peter to come to Caesarea. Accustomed to giving and obeying orders, the centurion sent immediately for three of his men. He told them of the vision, gave them directions, and asked them to hurry.

PETER'S VISION (10:9–16)

At noon the next day, after a busy morning of preaching, healing, and debating with the Jews, Peter retreated to his host's house for prayer, rest, and food. On the roof of the house, while

Cornelius

A centurion in the Roman army who lived at Caesarea. Although he was a Gentile, he was a worshiper of the one true God. He also treated the Jewish people with kindness and generosity. After an angel appeared to this pious soldier, he sent to Joppa for Simon Peter, who came to him with the message of forgiveness of sins through faith in the crucified and risen Christ. Cornelius became a Christian as a result of this incident. His conversion marked the beginning of the church's missionary activity among Gentiles. It also helped set the stage for an important early controversy in the church, for it raised the question of the possibility of salvation for those who were not Jews.

the meal was being prepared downstairs, Peter prayed and fell into a trance.

The heavens opened, and something like a huge sheet was let down. On the sheet were all kinds of animals and birds, ritually clean and unclean. A voice from heaven commanded Peter to rise, kill from among the animals, and satisfy his hunger. Peter was perplexed by the vision and protested vigorously. What the voice had requested was strictly against the Law.

Peter's reply was, "Surely not, Lord! I have never eaten anything impure or unclean." Why didn't Peter kill one of the clean animals? Because the clean animals had been defiled by coming into contact with unclean creatures. Then came the clincher from God. "Do not call anything impure that God has made clean." Peter saw this vision three times, and then the sheet was taken back to heaven.

Clean and Unclean Animals

In Leviticus 11, Moses and Aaron give both principles and specific instructions concerning animals which can be eaten and those which can't.

One such principle is: Whatever has a divided hoof and chews its cud can be eaten. A rock badger chews its cud but doesn't have a divided hoof, so it couldn't be eaten. A pig, on the other hand, has a divided hoof but doesn't chew its cud, so for that reason it wasn't to be eaten.

By this stage in his ministry, Peter's prejudices were being dealt with one by one. Already he had experienced many startling encounters with Samaritans, Hellenist Jews, and even some Gentiles. Those whom he had met, who had come to faith in Christ, gave undeniable evidence of a life-changing experience with Jesus—the same kind of experience that Peter was realizing. So Peter was making progress in working through his prejudices, but he was far from liberated. The fisherman would need all the spiritual help he could get as he dealt with Cornelius.

■ *God was preparing Peter for his meeting*
■ *with Cornelius, a Gentile. Jews and Gentiles*
■ *rarely ate together because Gentiles could*

Caesarea

Located on the Mediterranean Sea twenty-three miles south of Mount Carmel is the city of Caesarea. It is also known as Caesarea of Judea. After A.D 6 it became the official home of the Roman procurators. Hostilities between the Jewish and Gentile populations apparently had been a way of life in this city.

The city appears in the Book of Acts as a place of witness, travel, and the seat of government. Philip, having witnessed to the Ethiopian eunuch, is mentioned as arriving at Caesarea after a preaching mission. Peter led a centurion, Cornelius, who was stationed there to become a Christian. Paul had several reported contacts with the city as a port, and perhaps as a place of imprisonment and trial. Herod Agrippa I had a residence there and died there.

- *not be relied upon to eat only those foods that*
- *were "clean." Peter's vision denied any dis-*
- *tinction between "clean" and "unclean."*

PETER'S VISIT WITH CORNELIUS'S MESSENGERS (10:17–23)

Peter had no sooner awakened from his vision than the messengers arrived to request his visit to Cornelius. He welcomed his guests and provided lodging for them.

- *This passage affirms the power of God to*
- *break down even the strongest barriers of*
- *prejudice.*

PETER TRAVELS TO CAESAREA (10:23–33)

The next morning Peter, the messengers from Cornelius, and several Jewish Christians from Joppa set out for Caesarea.

After telling his story, Cornelius then requested Peter to bear witness to the gospel before the gathering of Gentiles.

PETER'S WITNESS AT CAESAREA (10:34–43)

Peter declared that "God does not show favoritism" in that He offers Himself to all men who will fear God and do what is right.

In line with other examples of apostolic preaching, Peter told his Gentile congregation that even though Jesus did good and was well beloved, the Jewish leaders killed Him by hanging Him on a tree. But He did not stay dead because God raised Him from death.

Peter closed with his personal affirmation of Jesus as judge of the living and the dead and the one about whom all the prophets had been speaking for centuries.

■ *Peter's sermon focused on his role as apos-*
■ *tolic witness to the entire ministry of*
■ *Jesus—above all to His death and resurrec-*
■ *tion. His key point was that God accepts peo-*
■ *ple of all races who respond in faith to the*
■ *gospel message.*

THE IMPARTIALITY OF THE SPIRIT (10:44–48)

Peter's preaching, coupled with the willingness of the Gentiles, opened the way for the Spirit of God to come to Cornelius and his company. As they listened to Peter's words about forgiveness for everyone who believes in Christ, the Holy Spirit suddenly descended upon all the Gentiles assembled in Cornelius's house. It was an audible, visible, objective demonstration of the Spirit's coming upon them. The Jewish Christians who had come from Joppa to witness the encounter were amazed to see the manifestation of the Spirit among these Romans.

Peter spent several days with his new Christian brothers and sisters in Caesarea. This inevitably involved table fellowship, but that now presented no problem for Peter. It would, however, constitute a major difficulty for more conservative Christians of Jewish background in Jerusalem.

Peter had already shown his own hesitancy to reach out to the Gentiles. More conservative elements in Jerusalem would be even more hesitant. Only an undeniable demonstration of divine power could overrule all objections, and God provided precisely that in Cornelius's house. Peter called for the baptism of the Gentiles and their full inclusion into the Christian community. This event illustrates a salvation truth: we cannot separate a Christian's confession of faith from the reception of the Spirit. The only valid salvation experience must include both.

Peter's Argument

1. The Holy Spirit came on the Gentiles just as He did on us.
2. Jesus said that John baptized with water but you will be baptized by means of the Holy Spirit.
3. Therefore, since God has given the Gentiles the same gift as he gave us, "who was I that I would be able to hinder God?" (Wuest)
Acts 11:15–18

■ *The gift of the Spirit had now been given to*
■ *the Gentiles in what has often been described*
■ *as the "Gentile Pentecost." This was a reve-*
■ *lation to Peter, who now accepted Gentiles as*
■ *part of the Christian community.*

QUESTIONS TO GUIDE YOUR STUDY

1. What did the conversion of Cornelius signify?
2. Why did God give Peter the vision in verses 9–16? How did the vision impact Peter?
3. What was the key point of Peter's sermon at Cornelius's house?

ACTS 11

The events in Caesarea were soon reported to the Jerusalem church. The Jewish Christians accused Peter not of preaching improperly but of going "into the house of uncircumcised men" and eating with them.

PETER'S REPORT (11:1–18)

Peter responded by recounting the events surrounding the conversion of Cornelius, including his vision and the presence of the Spirit. The testimony of Peter and his six companions convinced those in Jerusalem. They rejoiced that God was calling the Gentiles to repentance and life.

■ *Luke's message with this narrative of Peter's*
■ *report to Jerusalem is that no one can oppose*
■ *God or the spread of His gospel.*

ANTIOCH'S WITNESS TO GENTILES (11:19–30)

Chapter 11 as a whole is devoted to the foundational events in the Gentile mission of the church. Two different churches play the primary roles. One was the Jerusalem church, led by the Apostles and comprised mainly of Aramaic-speaking Jewish Christians. It recognized the divine leading in Peter's witness to Cornelius and concluded that God intended to lead the Gentiles to repentance and life.

The second was the Antioch church, established by Hellenists, those Greek-speaking Jewish Christians who had to flee Jerusalem after the martyrdom of Stephen. This church began to take to heart Peter's work and reach out to the Gentile population.

Antioch of Syria

Antioch was the third largest city in the Roman Empire—after Rome and Alexandria. It was founded on the Orontes River around 300 B.C. by Seleucus Nicator. From the beginning it was a bustling maritime city with its own seaport. It was located nearly three hundred miles north of Jerusalem and became home for many Jews of the Diaspora. Many of Antioch's Gentiles were attracted to Judaism.

Advance at Antioch (vv. 19–21)

By cooperating with the Lord, hundreds of people in Antioch came to faith in Jesus Christ and formed themselves into a strong church. Indeed, the Antioch church quickly became the great beachhead for launching the mission to the Gentiles. Further along in Luke's narrative, we find Paul adopting the Antioch church as his spiritual home.

Barnabas Sent to Antioch (vv. 22–24)

The Jerusalem church sent Barnabas to investigate reports of the overwhelming success of the gospel in Antioch. No doubt he eagerly accepted the assignment to investigate the Antioch church, rejoicing when he saw God living in the believers in Antioch. While he was in Antioch, he exhorted the church members to be faithful. Because of his preaching, even more people came to faith.

Barnabas Enlists Saul (vv. 25–26)

With the growing missionary success in Antioch, Barnabas needed help, and Paul immediately came to mind. Paul was in the area of his native Cilicia, to which he had departed after his first visit to Jerusalem following his conversion. When Barnabas finally located Paul, he brought him back to Antioch, where the two were heavily occupied in preaching and teaching in "great numbers."

Sending Famine Relief to Jerusalem (vv. 27–30)

Famine in Jerusalem

Luke dated the famine in Jerusalem squarely within the chronology of the Roman Empire. In fact, Luke's dating of this empire-wide famine within the reign of Claudius has been confirmed by a number of other ancient sources, including the Roman historian Suetonius. Luke's main reason for mentioning the famine, though, was to show that the Gentile Christians in Antioch participated in the famine relief effort.

One of the gifts of the Spirit to the church was that of prophecy. Perhaps men who felt this gift banded together into a "school of prophets" reminiscent of such groups in the Old Testament. A group of these men came to Antioch.

One of these men, Agabus, predicted a famine, which did occur. The church in Antioch, evidently spared the worst of the famine, collected funds to send to the mother church in Jerusalem for relief of suffering.

■ *The church at Antioch represented another*
■ *step in the movement of the gospel beyond*
■ *Judea and Syria. It was in Antioch that the*
■ *disciples were first called Christians.*

QUESTIONS TO GUIDE YOUR STUDY

1. When Peter reported to the Jerusalem Christians, what was their response?

2. What were the characteristics of the church at Antioch? How did they respond to the inclusion of Gentiles into the church?

3. Describe the ministry of Barnabas. What was his role in the early church?

ACTS 12 · · · · · · · · · · · · · · · · ·

HEROD AGRIPPA'S PERSECUTION OF THE APOSTLES (12:1–5)

Herod Agrippa I

About the time the Antioch church was preparing its relief offering for the Jerusalem church, during Herod touched off another round of persecution. This time the persecution of Christians was as much political as religious, since Herod could hardly have been considered a religious man. Such a persecution could have had religious motivations, though, if only for the political attempt to please the Jewish authorities. James, the brother of John, and one of the pillars of the Jerusalem church, was executed. Peter was arrested. Luke tells the martyrdom of James with the utmost brevity. He apparently did not want to dwell on it, but used the incident to set the stage for his main emphasis—God's deliverance of Peter.

Herod was the name given to the family which ruled Palestine immediately before and to some degree during the first half of the first Christian century. Their family was complex, and what information has come down has been frequently meager, conflicting, and difficult to harmonize. The chief sources are New Testament references, the Jewish historian Flavius Josephus, and a few obscure references by Roman historians such as Dio Cassius, Plutarch, and Strabo. Herod Agrippa I was the son of Aristobulus and grandson of Herod. He ruled with the title of king from A.D 41–44.

■ *Herod Agrippa initiated a round of persecu-*
■ *tion of the Apostles, with significant results.*

Prisons in the New Testament

The situation for prisoners was dismal in New Testament times, and concern for such persons was a virtue expected by Christ of every disciple (Matt. 25:36, 39, 43–44). Many New Testament characters were imprisoned for various reasons. John the Baptist was arrested for criticizing Herod Antipas. Peter was held under heavy security, consisting of chains, multiple guards, and iron doors. Paul, who imprisoned others, was often in prison himself. His experiences provide the most detail on prisons in the New Testament. In Philippi, he and Silas were placed under the charge of a lone jailer, who "put them in the inner cell and fastened their feet in the stocks" (Acts 16:24).

■ *James, the brother of John, was executed and*
■ *Peter was arrested and imprisoned.*

PETER'S MIRACULOUS DELIVERANCE FROM PRISON (12:6–19A)

Peter was anticipating a fate similar to that of James as he awaited his trial. Herod commanded that Peter be guarded by four squads of four soldiers each. Herod's plans, however, were thwarted by God's deliverance of Peter from prison.

Suddenly an angel of the Lord appeared, and a flash of heavenly light filled the cell. Peter was fast asleep, and the angel had to arouse him. Not fully alert, Peter had no idea what was happening. The angel told him to put on his coat and sandals. Peter was totally passive throughout the entire incident. His "escape" was truly a *deliverance*.

The scene shifts to the Christian community that had been praying fervently for Peter. He arrived at the house of Mary, mother of John Mark, and knocked on the door. Rhoda, a servant girl, answered and excitedly announced, "Peter is at the door!" Ironically, no one in this story was able to believe that Peter had been delivered from prison. Those gathered at the house of Mary and John Mark were unwilling to believe that Peter had escaped, even though their purpose for gathering had been to pray for Peter's release.

Verse 17 provides us with three important pieces of information: (1) Peter's report of his miraculous deliverance, (2) his instruction to tell the news to James, and (3) his departure to "another place," where he would find refuge from the wrath of Agrippa.

The guards who had been watching Peter could not have prevented his release. But Herod, in his madness, had them executed when told of the escape.

■ *The fervent prayer of the church led to Peter's*
■ *miraculous release from prison. Ironically,*
■ *they were surprised that Peter was delivered.*

HEROD'S DEATH (12:19B–23)

There are two climaxes to the account of Herod's persecution. One is Peter's escape from his clutches. The other is Herod's own grisly fate. Chronologically, his death came anywhere from several months to a year after Peter's escape. Christians viewed it very much as a divine retribution for what they had suffered under the king.

The quarreling cities of Tyre and Sidon were celebrating the restoration of their relations. A festival was declared. Herod wore a garment made of silver that glistened in the morning sun. As Herod, in all his glory, turned and addressed the people, they shouted, "This is the voice of a god, not of a man." Immediately he was struck down by the angel of the Lord, and was eaten by worms. He died five days later, according to the historian Josephus.

■ *This first major section of Luke ends with the*
■ *death of Herod Agrippa I. Luke implied that*
■ *Herod's death was related to his persecution*
■ *of Jewish Christians.*

A PEACE FOR THE CHURCH (12:24–25)

With Agrippa's sudden removal, the persecution of the church ended, and once more the word of God flourished.

QUESTIONS TO GUIDE YOUR STUDY

1. Describe the political climate of Herod Agrippa's reign. How did the church react to his persecution?
2. How did the praying Christians respond to the news that Peter had been delivered from prison? What lessons might we draw from this story?
3. Why did God strike down Herod Agrippa?

ACTS 13

Chapters 13 and 14 begin the story of the mission to the "ends of the earth." The Gentile mission, Paul's first missionary journey, started with Paul and Barnabas's work on Cyprus and in the Roman province of Galatia.

PAUL AND BARNABAS COMMISSIONED (13:1–3)

Acts portrays Paul as the great missionary, blazing trails for Christianity in areas that had never heard the gospel. Antioch served as a base from which Paul's journeys began, and he maintained close ties to the believers there throughout his missionary career.

The missionary call came to Paul and Barnabas while they worshiped with the church. The revelation that came was interpreted as being directly from the Spirit. The congregation responded in faith. The Spirit's command to call and commission Paul and Barnabas was quickly obeyed.

Barnabas

Barnabas was a Levite and a native of the island of Cyprus. His name was Joseph before the disciples called him Barnabas. The name Barnabas means "son of encouragement." And he lived up to his name. He was an active participant in the spread of the gospel. He sold his property and gave the proceeds to the Jerusalem church (Acts 4:36–37). He introduced Saul of Tarsus to the Jerusalem church (9:26–27).

- *When Paul and Barnabas heard their call,*
- *they were at church, and the congregation*
- *became a part of the total experience. To show*
- *their approval as well as to give their blessing,*
- *the congregation laid hands on these believers*
- *and sent them out on their mission.*

SERGIUS PAULUS CONVERTED ON CYPRUS (13:4–12)

The evangelization of Cyprus paralleled that of Samaria. Paul and the gospel had to overcome opposition from practitioners of magic. Elymas the sorcerer was as formidable an opponent for Paul as Simon Magnus had been for Peter. In Elymas, Paul faced not only the threat of magic but that of Jewish opposition as well. Paul's triumph in this event showed the power of the gospel (and the Spirit) to deal with any opposition, especially that of magic. This event also resulted in faith on the part of the Roman proconsul, Sergius Paulus. Finally, almost as a footnote, Luke mentions that Saul's other name was Paul. (Saul apparently Latinized his name to Paul, by which he is called throughout the rest of his life.) Up to this point, Luke had referred to Paul by his Hebrew name Saul, without any indication of Paul's social status. As Paul moved closer to the center of the Roman Empire, Luke switched names.

Paul's First Missionary Journey

Paul's first penetration into the Gentile world began in Antioch in Syria and took him to the island of Cyprus and the mainland cities of Perga, Antioch in Pisidia, Iconium, Lystra, and Derbe. After reaching Derbe, Paul reversed his travels, returning through the cities he had just visited, and finally departing from the port of Attalia for the return to Antioch of Syria.

Paul's missionary policy involved entering a city, establishing a foundation among the residents who responded to his preaching, and moving to another city under pressure from local authorities or other evident signs of divine leadership. Barnabas accompanied Paul throughout this first journey, and John Mark served as a coworker for a portion of the trip.

(See map of "Paul's First Missionary Journey" on p. 50)

- *Paul's triumph in showing the power of the*
- *gospel to deal with opposition, especially*
- *magic, resulted in faith on the part of the*
- *Roman proconsul, Sergius Paulus.*

The Setting (vv. 13–16a)

The remainder of Acts 13 is set primarily in Pisidian Antioch. It consists of three main parts: (1) Paul's journey to Antioch and the setting of the stage for Paul's speech in the synagogue, (2) Paul's address to the synagogue, and (3) the final response of the Jews and Gentiles on the occasion of a second visit to the synagogue in Antioch.

Paul's Address to the Synagogue at Pisidian Antioch (13:16b–41)

This is Paul's first recorded sermon. It has much in common with Peter's speechs—the emphasis on the Jewish leaders' responsibility for Jesus' death, the contrast between the death on the cross and the triumph of the Resurrection, the apostolic witness, the proofs from Scripture (even some of the same texts). This sermon has a feature in common also with Stephen's speech, namely, the introductory sketch of Jewish history. Whereas Stephen used Old Testament history to depict the rebellion of the Jews toward divinely appointed leaders, Paul used it to show God's faithfulness to His promises for Israel—promises that were ultimately fulfilled in Christ.

"God-fearers" were Gentile believers in God, practitioners of Judaism, but not full-fledged converts. Paul emphasized that the Jews were chosen people, not because of their merit but because of God's grace.

Paul addressed the men of Israel and the God-fearers.

■ *Paul's presentation was designed to prove*
■ *that Jesus was the Messiah who had been*
■ *promised in the Old Testament, that Jesus*
■ *had been crucified and raised from the dead,*
■ *and that forgiveness of sins was being offered*
■ *through Christ.*

THE SERMON'S AFTERMATH (13:42–52)

Paul's synagogue audience was at first favorably impressed by what he had to say. He was so effective, in fact, that many "followed Paul and Barnabas" and "almost the whole city" returned to hear him on the next Sabbath. The Jewish leaders responded to Paul's popularity with jealousy and abuse. Because the Jews had rejected the gospel, Paul and Barnabas made it clear that the gospel would be given to the Gentiles.

■ *Paul and the Christian church often strug-*
■ *gled to convince people their worship was*
■ *different from other religious ceremonies.*
■ *Therefore, when the Jews incited God-fear-*
■ *ing women and leading men of the city, that*
■ *posed a serious problem for Paul and Barna-*
  bas.

QUESTIONS TO GUIDE YOUR STUDY

1. What did overcoming Elymas the sorcerer show the people of Cyprus?
2. What was the point of Paul's address to the Jews at Pisidian Antioch?
3. Describe how the Jewish crowd responded to Paul's sermon?

ACTS 14

ACCEPTANCE AND REJECTION AT ICONIUM (14:1–7)

Paul and Barnabas left Antioch of Pisidia to go eastward to Iconium. They began their work in

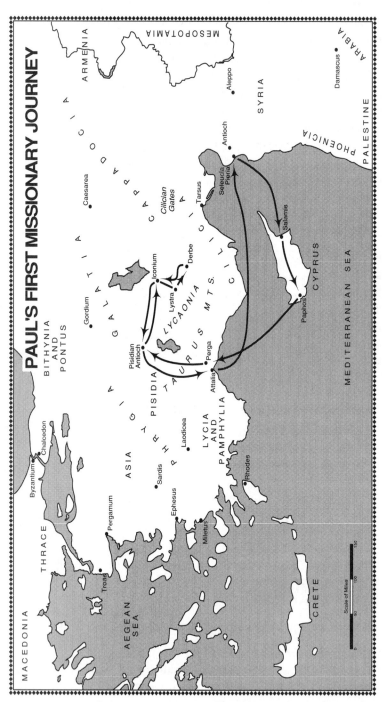

PAUL'S FIRST MISSIONARY JOURNEY

Taken from John B. Polhill, Acts , vol. 26, New American Commentary (Nashville, Tenn.: Broadman & Holman Publishers, 1992) p. 58.

the synagogue, but opposition grew. Again, the Jews tried to stir up the Gentiles to have Paul and Barnabas stoned. The missionaries discovered the plot and fled to the southern part of the province of Galatia, to Lystra and Derbe.

- *Paul followed the pattern of establishing a witness in the major population centers.*
- *While in Iconium, Paul and Barnabas took their message to both Jews and Gentiles.*
- *After discovering a plot by authorities to kill them, they fled to nearby Lystra and Derbe.*

PREACHING TO PAGANS AT LYSTRA (14:8–21a)

A Lame Man Healed (vv. 8–10)

While at Lystra, Paul healed a crippled man. The healing of this man has many features in common with Peter's healing of Aeneas (9:32–35) and particularly with his healing of the lame man at the temple gate. Like the latter, this man had been lame from birth. Also like the man at the temple, this man leaped up and walked about when healed.

Paul and Barnabas Paid Homage (vv. 11–13)

This event precipitated a remarkable reaction from the native Lystrans, who attempted to honor the Apostles as gods. "The gods have come down to us in human form!" they exclaimed. The crowd then wanted to offer sacrifices to them—thinking Paul was Hermes and Barnabas was Zeus.

Paul and Barnabas Dismayed (vv. 14–18)

This reaction prompted a strong response from Paul and Barnabas, which was expressed in the

Iconium

Iconium was a city in Asia Minor. Paul endured suffering and persecution at Iconium (2 Tim. 3:11). Its location is that of the modern Turkish provincial capital of Konya. Iconium was mentioned for the first time in the fourth century B.C. by the historian Xenophon. In New Testament times it was considered part of the Roman province of Galatia. Evidently it has had a continuous existence since its founding.

Hermes and Zeus

Since Paul was doing most of the speaking, they thought he was Hermes—the Greek god of eloquence and messenger of all the other gods. They took Barnabas to be Zeus, the king of the Greek gods. According to an ancient legend, Zeus and Hermes once came to earth as humans. Archaeologists have discovered inscriptions in this region dedicated to Zeus and Hermes.

tearing of their clothes and in a sermon which followed (vv. 14–18). Paul exhorted them to abandon their vain worship and turn to the one true and living God, the source of all that lives. Paul emphasized three things about God:

1. God is the Creator of all life.
2. God is forbearing and merciful.
3. God had revealed Himself in acts of natural providence.

Paul begins with well-known elements of life for these Gentiles—

1. Rain from heaven.
2. Crops in their seasons.
3. Abundance of food which gives joy.

He then says, in effect, let me tell you about the One who provides all of this for you. In spite of this effort, Luke says that Paul and Barnabas had difficulty keeping the crowd from sacrificing to them.

Paul and Barnabas Rejected (vv. 19–20a)

Ironically, the ministry at Lystra concluded when the crowd turned against Paul and tried to stone him to death. Jews from Antioch and Iconium, having followed Paul to Lystra, stirred up the crowd who then stoned Paul and left him for dead.

Luke's matter-of-fact narration observes that other believers surrounded Paul to formed a hedge around him as they returned to the city. This must have been a great encouragement to the believers and a great surprise to those who thought they had killed Paul.

Paul and Barnabas did not linger in Lystra, as it was no longer safe. The next morning they set out for Derbe.

■ *The fickle crowds, filled with propaganda*
■ *from Jews who arrived in Lystra from Anti-*
■ *och and Iconium, turned against Paul and*
■ *apparently joined in stoning him. Paul, left*
■ *for dead by the vengeful mob, revived,*
■ *returned to Lystra, and departed to preach in*
■ *Derbe, over fifty miles from Lystra.*

THE MINISTRY AT DERBE (14:20b–21a)

Luke provides only the essential details that a successful witness took place at Derbe, and that many disciples were won to the Lord. Derbe was the easternmost church established on this mission by Paul and Barnabas.

THE MISSIONARIES RETURN TO ANTIOCH (14:21b–28)

Paul and Barnabas ended their mission work by retracing their steps to visit all the churches that had been established. Importantly, they "appointed elders" for each of the churches.

Derbe

Derbe was an important city in the region of Lycaonia in the province of Galatia in Asia Minor. It was apparently near what is modern Kerti Huyuk. The residents of Derbe and Lystra spoke a different language than the people to the north in Iconium. Paul visited Derbe on his first missionary journey, fleeing from Iconium. Persecution in Lystra led to a successful preaching mission in Derbe. On the second missionary journey, Paul returned to Derbe. He apparently visited again on the third journey. Paul's fellow minister Gaius was from Derbe.

■ *The missionary journey ended where it*
■ *began, at Antioch of Syria. Paul and Barna-*
■ *bas reported all that had happened in Asia*
■ *Minor, with special emphasis on the way*
■ *God "had opened the door of faith to the Gen-*
■ *tiles."*

QUESTIONS TO GUIDE YOUR STUDY

1. How did the people of Iconium treat Paul and Barnabas? What was usually at the core of Jewish opposition?

2. What were the three main truths in Paul's sermon to the pagans at Lystra?

3. As Paul and Barnabas completed their mission, they retraced their steps on the return trip. What did they do to help strengthen church leadership when they revisited the various churches?

ACTS 15

Acts 15:1–35 stands at the very center of the Book of Acts. Not only is this the midpoint in the narrative, but it is also central in the development of the narrative's total plot. The first half of Acts focused on the Jewish community, particularly the influential Jerusalem church. The Christian witness had begun there. Believers took all the preliminary steps for a major effort to reach the Gentile world. The stage was now set for Paul's mission to the heart of the Greco-Roman world as *the* missionary to the Gentiles.

DEBATE IN JERUSALEM OVER ACCEPTANCE OF THE GENTILES (15:1–35)

This section falls into four natural parts: the introduction, the debate in Jerusalem, the final solution, and the debate's conclusion.

The Criticism from the Circumcision Party (vv. 1–5)

There were many Gentiles in the church at Antioch. There is no indication that they had been circumcised when they joined the Christian fellowship. This was disturbing to some Jewish Christians who came from Judea and insisted that circumcision was necessary for salvation.

The Debate in Jerusalem (vv. 6–21)

There were two major witnesses, both in defense of the view that the Gentiles should not be burdened by circumcision and the Law. Peter spoke first, followed by James. Luke precedes both speeches with brief summaries that set the context of the conference.

Peter's speech reminded the group of the work of the Spirit in the conversion of the first Gentile, Cornelius. Paul and Barnabas also referred to the miraculous work of God in their experiences with the Gentiles. To James was left the final statement.

The Decision in Jerusalem (vv. 22–29)

James, the half brother of Jesus, had come to be recognized as the leader of the church in Jerusalem. After the debate and testimonies, James gave his decision, which was subsequently ratified by the assembly. James, speaking courageously and against the prevailing spirit of the Jerusalem church, maintained that Gentile Christians should not be weighed down with Jewish customs. But, rather, for their own souls' good health, they should abstain from food offered to idols, avoid all sexual unchastity, and eat nothing strangled. The dietary regulations are attempts at compromise. It is as if James said, "We have freed you from circumcision. Help us save face a bit by observing these basic, painless food restrictions."

The decision pleased them all, and by common consent the council and Jerusalem congregation selected emissaries who would travel to the Gentile churches to give word of liberation.

Jesus' Brothers

During Jesus' ministry the brothers of Jesus were not believers. Paul specifically mentioned a Resurrection appearance by Jesus to James (1 Cor. 15:7). After the Resurrection and Ascension, Jesus' brothers are said to have been with the twelve and the other believers in Jerusalem (Acts 1:14).

John Mark

John Mark was an early missionary and church leader. He is the author of the Gospel of Mark. He was the son of Mary in whose home the Jerusalem believers met to pray when Peter was imprisoned by Herod Agrippa I (Acts 12:12). Mark was sometimes called by his Jewish name, John, and sometimes by his Roman name, Mark. He was a cousin of Barnabas (Col. 4:10). After Barnabas and Paul completed a relief mission to Jerusalem, they took Mark with them when they returned to Antioch. When Barnabas and Paul went as missionaries, they took Mark to help. They went from Antioch to Cyprus and then on to Pamphylia, where Mark left them and returned to Jerusalem (13:13).

The most likely reason for his leaving was because Paul had become dominant and was taking the gospel to the Gentiles.

■ *James's decision stated that Gentiles would*
■ *not be hindered from becoming Christians;*
■ *they would not be required to undergo cir-*
■ *cumcision. Practically, however, the council*
■ *requested that Gentile Christians refrain*
■ *from practices that would put a strain on*
■ *their relationship with Jewish Christians.*

The Decision Reported to Antioch (vv. 30–35)

Antioch was the first recorded stop on the good news tour. Silas and Barsabbas, who were appointed by the Jerusalem church, read the letter, gave details of the decision. Amid much rejoicing, the Antioch group received the good news.

The Jerusalem council marks the culmination of the first missionary journey and serves as the catalyst for the second missionary journey. The impetus for the second journey was the reading of the apostolic letter prepared by the Jerusalem council to the churches in Asia Minor. If Paul needed a reason to strike again, the urgency to deliver the letter and interpret its intentions was all that was necessary.

See "Paul's Missionary Journeys Harmonized with the Pauline Epistles" on page 111 for summary information about Paul's first missionary journey.

PAUL PARTS COMPANY WITH BARNABAS (15:36–41)

Paul Proposes Another Trip (v. 36)

"Some time" later Paul suggested to Barnabas that they revisit "all the towns" where they had established churches on their first mission. The imprecise time expression is perhaps significant as Luke's way of marking a major new division in the narrative.

Disagreement over John Mark (vv. 37–38)

Paul and Barnabas agreed to part ways. The reason for their going separate ways was not a happy one and involved a major disagreement between them. John Mark was the center of contention. He was Barnabas's cousin, and Barnabas had suggested that he accompany them as he had on their first mission (13:5). Paul did not think this a wise move since Mark had abandoned them on that occasion (v. 13). There may also have been a personality clash between Paul and John Mark.

For whatever reason, Paul and Barnabas were in sharp disagreement. Failing to resolve both the issue and feelings, their only course of action was to separate.

Paul and Silas (vv. 39–41)

Paul needed a suitable replacement for a traveling companion and chose Silas. Paul and Silas headed north from Antioch by foot and visited the churches of Syria and Cilicia along the way.

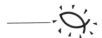

Paul and John Mark Reconciled

When Paul wrote Philemon, Mark was one of Paul's fellow workers who sent greetings. Paul wrote to the Colossians to receive Mark should he came to them (Col. 4:10). When Paul wrote his final letter to Timothy, he asked Timothy to bring Mark with him because Paul considered Mark a useful helper.

Silas

Silas was a leader in the early Jerusalem church. He accompanied both Peter and Paul on separate missionary journeys. One of his first missions was to carry news of the Jerusalem conference to the believers in Antioch.

- *After a disagreement on traveling companions,*
- *Paul and Barnabas parted company. As a result,*
- *Barnabas and Mark decided to travel to Cyprus,*
- *and Paul and Silas were to begin the second*
- *journey through Asia Minor and Greece.*

QUESTIONS TO GUIDE YOUR STUDY

1. Describe the debate that took place in Jerusalem. What was the issue that needed a resolution?

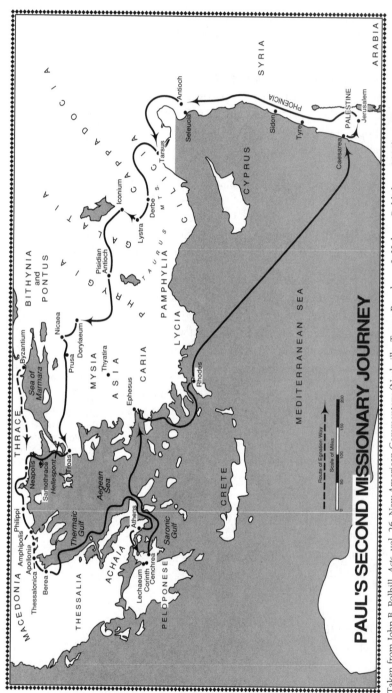

PAUL'S SECOND MISSIONARY JOURNEY

Taken from John B. Polhill, *Acts*, vol. 26, New American Commentary (Nashville, Tenn.: Broadman & Holman Publishers, 1992), p. 59

2. How did James resolve the issue? How did the assembly respond to his decision?

3. Why did Paul and Barnabas part ways? Do you think this split helped or hurt the church's missionary efforts?

ACTS 16

REVISITING DERBE, LYSTRA, AND ICONIUM (16:1–5)

Paul's first evangelistic tour went as far as Lystra and Derbe. When Paul and Barnabas left that area of Asia Minor, on their first trip, the Jews were so opposed to their ministry that the missionaries had been forced to leave hurriedly. Paul's stated purpose for this trip was to strengthen the churches that had been established in the earlier journey. The focus of his visit to Lystra, however, was on Timothy, a young disciple who came to faith in Christ on Paul's first visit there.

Paul accepted the recommendation of the believers in the area and took Timothy as a companion. Paul circumcised Timothy to make Timothy acceptable to Jewish Christians.

■ *Paul's first evangelistic tour went as far as*
■ *Lystra and Derbe. Paul's stated purpose for*
■ *this trip was to strengthen the churches that*
■ *had been established in the earlier journey.*

Timothy

Personal name meaning "honoring God." When he was a child, his mother Eunice and his grandmother Lois taught him the Scriptures. A native of Lystra, he may have been converted on Paul's first missionary journey. By the time Paul came back to Lystra, Timothy had become so well respected, Paul invited him to accompany him. Since Timothy's father was Greek, Timothy had not been circumcised at birth.

CALLED TO MACEDONIA (16:6–10)

Paul, Silas, and Timothy now headed north, probably from Pisidian Antioch through

Phrygia and Galatia. But God had other plans for the missionaries. The Spirit prevented them from entering the Roman province called Asia. Unable to preach in Asia, the small company prepared to go into Bithynia, but once again they were prevented by the Spirit.

God sent a vision to Paul, perhaps a dream in the middle of the night. A man of Macedonia appeared, begging him to come and witness to the Macedonians. Paul realized this vision was God's way of calling him to a mission in Macedonia.

■ *Twice the Spirit guided the movement of the*
■ *gospel. Rather than moving toward the*
■ *northern part of Asia Minor, as Paul desired,*
■ *the gospel was pointed toward the Western*
■ *world.*

THE "WE" PASSAGES

At this point (16:10), the narrative changes from third person to first person. This begins one of the "we" passages in Acts which begins and ends with Philippi. The second of the "we" section begins again when the missionaries return to Philippi (20:5–15). One possible explanation for this is that Luke was part of Paul's vision and a resident of Philippi.

WITNESSING IN PHILIPPI (16:11–40)

The remainder of this chapter concerns Paul's work in Philippi. It falls into four separate scenes.

Founding a Church with Lydia (vv. 11–15)

Philippi had such a small Jewish population that the city lacked the ten Jewish men necessary to build a synagogue. Among the women who had gathered for prayer, Lydia, a businesswoman from Thyatira, was the one responsive to the gospel. Her offer of hospitality to Paul and his missionary team demonstrated the reality of her conversion. She did not just open her home to the missionaries; she also allowed it to become the gathering place for the entire Christian community.

Lydia

Thyatira was a center of the purple dye business. Since purple goods were expensive, Lydia was likely a wealthy person—and one who had traveled far more than most women of her day.

Healing a Possessed Servant Girl (vv. 16–24)

Verse 16 opens a new scene but connects with the previous one to make a new narrative. On one of the occasions when the four missionaries were going outside the city to the place of prayer, they were encountered by a slave girl with a spirit by which she predicted the future.

Like the demoniacs during Jesus' ministry, the possessed girl was evidently able to see into the true nature of Paul's preaching, particularly into the reality of the God he proclaimed. She constantly followed the missionaries about, shouting that they were servants of the "Most High God, who are telling you the way to be saved." Paul, in a form reminiscent of Jesus' exorcisms, commanded the spirit to leave the girl. The spirit did so immediately.

But her masters, who exploited her condition, lost their source of income and became furious at Paul. Seeing their young fortune-teller well and whole, they dragged Paul and Silas before the magistrates who judged the city in the name of the Roman emperor.

Apparently, with little or no judicial hearing, Paul and Silas were stripped and beaten and then delivered to a prison keeper, who clapped them in stocks and locked them in a cell in the town dungeon.

The first-person narrative stops at verse 17 and does not reappear in Acts until Paul's return to Philippi in 20:6.

Converting a Prison Keeper's Household
(vv. 25–34)

This event falls into two divisions. The first relates to Paul and Silas's deliverance from prison. The second concerns the prison keeper and his household.

The Deliverance. It was the middle of the night. Paul and Silas were singing hymns of praise to God. As they sang and prayed, an earthquake shook the jail. The bars and doors flew open. Everyone's chains came loose. The chains perhaps attached to the walls, were wrenched loose by the quake's violence.

Prison keepers and guards were personally responsible for their prisoners and in some instances were executed for allowing them to escape.

The jailer was aroused by the earthquake and spotted the open door. Supposing the prisoners had already escaped, he drew his sword to kill himself, preferring death by his own hand rather than by Roman justice.

When Paul saw what the jailer was about to do, he shouted for him to stop, assuring him they were in their cell. The miraculous release did not lead to their escape but to a far more significant event—the jailer's conversion.

The Witness. Calling for lamps and torches, the jailer rushed in and fell at the feet of Paul and Silas. Paul had saved his life, and Paul's God, who had, in an instant, made ineffective all his efforts at prison security, was obviously the one to be respected. The jailer's response was, "Sirs, what must I do to be saved?"

The missionaries' response was, "Believe in the Lord Jesus, and you will be saved—you and your household." At some point, the prison keeper's household entered the scene. The whole family came to faith in God.

Humbling the City Magistrates (vv. 35–40)

The next day the magistrates decided that Paul and Silas had sufficiently paid for the crime of disturbing the peace. So, quite casually, they issued an order for their release. After all, they had been beaten and locked in the dungeon overnight—and all of that without a trial. It was strictly an illegal procedure. They had scourged and imprisoned two Roman citizens with no formal condemnation, and that was beyond their authority.

When the magistrates learned they had improperly treated and wrongly imprisoned Roman citizens, they became fearful. The magistrates who condemned Paul and Silas now found themselves genuine lawbreakers.

Paul insisted that the magistrates personally come to the prison and escort them out. The nervous magistrates entered the prison, escorted the prisoners out, and told them to leave town. Paul and Silas did leave, but only after they had spent some time with Lydia and other new converts in the city.

Paul's Roman Citizenship

Paul was not only "a Hebrew of the Hebrews" but a Roman citizen. Paul's rights as a Roman citizen come to the fore not only here but in Acts 22:24–29 when he was about to be beaten and in Acts 25:10–12 when he exercised his right to appeal to the Emperor.

■ *Part of the significance of the conversion of*
■ *the Philippian jailer is that this is the first*
■ *recorded episode of a person, with no prior*
■ *exposure to Judaism—an out-and-out*
■ *pagan—becoming a believer in Jesus Christ.*

QUESTIONS TO GUIDE YOUR STUDY

1. From the events of this chapter, describe how the Holy Spirit guided the movement of the gospel message.

2. Who was Lydia? How did she help the spread of Christianity into her community?

3. What was the result of Paul and Silas's witness to the prison keeper?

ACTS 17

Success in Thessalonica

Paul later wrote to the Thessalonians "You suffered much, but still you accepted the teaching with joy that comes from the Holy Spirit. So you became an example to all the believers in Macedonia and Southern Greece. And the Lord's teaching spread from you not only into Macedonia and Southern Greece, but now your faith in God has become known everywhere."
I Thess. 1:6b–8a

ESTABLISHING CHURCHES IN THESSALONICA AND BEREA (17:1–15)

Acceptance and Rejection in Thessalonica (vv. 1–9)

Paul, Silas, and Timothy proceeded from Philippi to the major seaport city of Thessalonica, sixty-two miles distant. Thessalonica was then (as now) the second largest city in Greece. Here Paul resumed the missionary pattern established in the first missionary journey. Again his ministry in the synagogue led to saving faith on the part of many Jews and Gentiles and opposition from leading Jewish citizens. As in Philippi, Paul and Silas were accused of insurrection, but they were released and asked to leave the city rather than being jailed.

Witness in Berea (vv. 10–15)

From Thessalonica the three missionaries went to Berea. Luke describes the Jews of Berea as being of "more noble character" than the Thessalonians. These people were open, tolerant, and generous. They took Paul's scriptural exposition seriously. They did their own examination of the Scriptures to see if they really did point to the death and Resurrection of the Messiah as Paul claimed. They met daily to search the Scriptures. It is no wonder so many contemporary Bible study groups call themselves "Bereans."

This ideal situation did not last forever. Although their reception initially was more favorable than at Thessalonica, Paul again was forced to leave because of opposition aroused by the Jews who had come from Thessalonica. Leaving Silas and Timothy behind, Paul headed south to Athens.

Perhaps the most interesting part of this passage is that in Berea, Greek men believed, as well as women.

In Paul's day, Athens was only a shadow of its former glory in its golden age in the fourth and fifth centuries B.C. Even the native population of Athens had dwindled, estimated at 5,000 voting citizens. That number was, however, considerably augmented by artists, students, and tourists in the city. It was still considered the cultural and intellectual center of the Roman Empire.

■ *In spite of opposition from local Jews, the*
■ *missionary team of Paul, Silas, and Timothy*
■ *established churches in the Greek cities of*
■ *Thessalonica and Berea.*

WITNESSING TO THE ATHENIAN INTELLECTUALS (17:16–34)

The Athenians' Curiosity (vv. 16–21)

In Athens, Paul reasoned with the Jews at the Synagogue. He also bore his witness in the Agora, the famous marketplace and hub of Athenian life. There he got his most pronounced response, especially from some of the philosophers.

The philosophers called Paul a "babbler." They did not understand Paul's concept of resurrection. Epicureans did not believe in any existence after death, and Stoics believed that only the soul, the divine spark, survived death. Their response to Paul's idea of resurrection was, "He seems to be advocating foreign gods."

"Babbler"

When the philosophers dubbed Paul a "babbler," they were not using a complimentary term. They used a colorful word *(spermologos)* meaning "seed-picker," which evokes images of a bird pecking indiscriminately at seeds in a barnyard. It referred to someone who picked up scraps of ideas here and there and passed them off as profound truth with no depth of understanding.

Areopagus

The Areopagus was the site of Paul's speech to the Epicurean and Stoic philosophers of Athens, Greece. It was a rocky hill about 370 feet high, not far from the Acropolis and the Agora (marketplace). The word was also used to refer to the council that originally met on this hill. The name probably was derived from Ares, the Greek name for the god of war known to the Romans as Mars.

Paul's Testimony before the Areopagus (vv. 22–31)

Paul's speech on the Areopagus was an attempt to present the gospel in a setting different from any Luke had described before. This speech is a masterpiece of Hellenistic rhetoric. Paul did not begin with the Old Testament; his starting point was Greek philosophy and literature. Paul had observed in the city an altar with the inscription: "to an unknown god." This gave him the perfect launching pad for his presentation.

Paul presented four God-centered themes in his speech:

The Creator God. Paul referred to God as the maker of the "world," a term familiar to every Greek. Once granted the premise that God is Creator, two things follow. First, God "does not live in temples built by hands." Second, God is totally self-sufficient and totally without need.

The Providential God. The verses of this section form the center of the speech. They contain two emphases: (1) God's providence over humanity and (2) human responsibility to God.

The Worship of God. This section is the basis for Paul's critique of idolatrous worship, and it provides the "scriptural base" for the speech. Scripture would have been meaningless to the Greeks, so Paul addressed them as much as possible in their own terms—just as he did the citizens of Lystra (14:15–17). If the Greeks had genuinely accepted Paul's major premise that God is Creator, they would have had to acknowledge their own idolatry and their own need for repentance.

The Judgment of God. Paul concluded that all people must ultimately stand before God and give an account of their relationship to Him. The clincher that brought Paul's discourse to an abrupt halt: the resurrection of the dead. With the mention of the resurrection, the jeering started. The party broke up on that statement.

The Mixed Response (vv. 32–34)

Some of the Greeks scoffed, while others wanted to hear Paul again. A few people responded in faith. One who did believe was a member of the inner circle of Areopagites, a man named Dionysius. Another convert is mentioned by name—Damaris, a woman.

■ *Paul's speech was unique in its appeal to*
■ *Greek philosophical thought. Paul held his*
■ *own, even in the midst of cynical intellectu-*
■ *alism. The result was that some people who*
■ *heard Paul were moved to salvation.*

QUESTIONS TO GUIDE YOUR STUDY

1. How did the Bereans receive Paul and Silas? What did they accomplish there?
2. What was Paul's message to the Greek pagans? What was their response?
3. Women were prominent in Paul's Greek congregations. What instances can you cite where women were instrumental in the spread of the gospel?

Corinth

Corinth was located on the southwest end of the isthmus that joined the southern part of the Greek peninsula with the mainland to the north.

Corinth was an important city long before it became a Roman colony in 44 B.C. In addition to the extant works of early writers, modern archaeology has contributed to knowledge of ancient Corinth.

Corinth in Paul's day was a cosmopolitan city composed of people from varying cultural backgrounds. Being near the site of the Isthmian games held every two years, the Corinthians enjoyed the pleasures of these games and the wealth which visitors brought to the city. Sailors would come to the city to spend their money on the pleasures of Corinth, which was especially known for its licentious lifestyle.

ACTS 18

ESTABLISHING A CHURCH IN CORINTH (18:1–17)

From Athens, Paul next traveled to Corinth, a major commercial center. In Paul's day, Corinth was the largest and most cosmopolitan city of Greece.

The Mission to Corinth (vv. 1–11)

From Luke's narrative, we know that Paul ministered here for about eighteen months. Three things about this passage are noteworthy. First is Paul's encounter with Aquila and Priscilla. In these Jewish Christians Paul found company and encouragement when he needed both. They, like him, were tentmakers.

Second, Paul went to the Jewish community in Corinth. They rejected his witness and became abusive. Paul shook out his clothes in protest and told them he had fulfilled his responsibility to them and they would have to live with the consequences of their guilt.

At Corinth Paul was free to witness freely, not just on Sabbaths. Second Corinthians 11:8–10 and Philippians 4:15–17 speak of support of other churches while Paul ministered in Corinth. (See page 111, "Paul's Missionary Journeys Harmonized with the Pauline Epistles.")

The Accusation before Gallio (vv. 12–17)

As a result of intensified attacks from some of the Jews in Corinth, Paul was brought before Gallio, the proconsul and charged with "persuading people to worship God in ways contrary to the law." Paul's appearance before Gallio is important in two respects. First, it established a precedent for the manner in which the Roman leaders should consider charges against Christians brought before them. Second, the mention of Gallio is an important reference point for determining the date of Paul's work in Corinth and for establishing the entire Pauline chronology.

- *Certain Jews, seeking to get Roman punish-*
- *ment of Paul charged him with advocating an*
- *unlawful religion. However, Gallio consid-*
- *ered Christianity to be part of Judaism and*
- *granted it all the rights and privileges enjoyed*
- *by the Jewish religion in the Roman Empire.*

RETURNING TO ANTIOCH (18:18–22)

This passage provides a transition between Paul's second and third missions. Capitalizing on the favorable judgment on the part of Gallio, Paul remained in Corinth for several more months, working day and night for the cause of Christ.

After his eighteen-month ministry at Corinth was completed, Paul and his companions (including Aquila and Priscilla) traveled to Ephesus. Paul left Aquila and Priscilla there while he returned to his home base, Antioch of Syria.

- *With Paul's return to Antioch, the stage was*
- *set for his third missionary journey. Aquila*
- *and Priscilla would carry on the witness in*
- *Ephesus until his return.*

APOLLOS IN EPHESUS (18:23–28)

In 18:24–28, Luke mentions the arrival in Ephesus of Apollos, an eloquent Jew from Alexandria.

Corinth was one of the four prominent centers in the New Testament account of the early church, the other three being Jerusalem, Antioch of Syria, and Ephesus. Paul's first extended ministry at one city was at Corinth. After he visited Corinth for the first time, he decided to remain here for at least eighteen months. Paul's three longest letters are associated with Corinth.

Gallio, as Roman provincial governor of Achaia, was headquartered in Corinth. Certain Jews brought Paul before Gallio, seeking to have him punished. They charged that Paul advocated an unlawful religion. Gallio considered Christianity to be part of Judaism, with all the rights and privileges the Jewish religion enjoyed in the Roman Empire. In fact, Gallio refused to take jurisdiction over the dispute.

Apollos

An educated man, Apollos handled Old Testament Scriptures with forcefulness. However, he lacked a full understanding of the way of God, so Priscilla and Aquila instructed him. Apollos became even more successful in his ministry. He greatly strengthened believers by using the Scriptures to demonstrate that Jesus was the Christ.

Apollos in Corinth

Some New Testament references compare Apollos with Paul or Peter (1 Cor. 1:12; 3:4–6, 22). In 1 Cor. 4:6, Paul placed Apollos on the same level as himself. He also referred to Apollos as his brother (1 Cor. 16:12). They both sought to defeat the arrogance and superiority that comes from being self-centered rather than Christ-centered. Because of Apollos's knowledge of the Old Testament, Luther suggested that Apollos might be the writer of the Book of Hebrews.

Apollos had a thorough knowledge of Scripture and spoke with fervor; however, he only knew of the baptism of John. After Priscilla and Aquila instructed him on this issue, Apollos traveled to the province of Achaia and the city of Corinth, where he provided significant help to those who had believed and also refuted unbelieving Jews.

- *Paul launched his third missionary journey.*
- *Meanwhile, in Ephesus, a young Alexandrian*
- *Jew named Apollos, well-educated in the Old*
- *Testament Scriptures, became a key figure in*
- *the spread of the gospel in the province of*
- *Achaia.*

QUESTIONS TO GUIDE YOUR STUDY

1. Describe the setting at Corinth. Why would many in this city oppose Paul's gospel message?
2. What strengths did Apollos bring to the leadership of the early church?
3. Describe the spread of the gospel to this point in Acts. Comment on how God orchestrated the varying personalities and events that contributed to its growth.

ACTS 19

Paul's third missionary journey parallels Jesus' passion narrative. Like Jesus, Paul turned his face to Jerusalem, where he was captured, taken before Jewish and Roman officials, and placed in Roman hands.

PAUL'S THIRD MISSIONARY JOURNEY

Alternative route

Route of Egnatian Way

Scale of Miles

0   50   100   150   200

Taken from John B. Polhill, Acts vol. 26, New American Commentary (Nashville, Tenn.: Broadman & Holman Publishers, 1992), p. 60.

Paul's Third Missionary Journey

Paul began his third missionary journey from Antioch. He traveled through Galatia and Phrygia, provinces he had visited on his previous missionary journeys. One of the key aims of this journey was to strengthen all the believers. Paul's third journey concluded with his arrival in Jerusalem in Acts 21:17.

PAUL'S WITNESS TO THE DISCIPLES OF JOHN THE BAPTIST (19:1–7)

When Paul arrived at Ephesus, he encountered some disciples of John the Baptist.

Paul's interrogation of these followers of John revealed that at no point had they advanced beyond John the Baptist's initial preaching of repentance, which was in preparation for the coming of the Messiah. In fact, they were unaware of the events of Pentecost. Paul asked them if they had received the Spirit. Their reply was, "We have not even heard that there is a Holy Spirit."

After prayer and the laying on of hands, the Spirit came to these disciples. They spoke in tongues and prophesied. As throughout Acts, there was no set pattern in the way this gift was bestowed. The Spirit came at various times and in various ways.

Occasions of the Spirit's Coming in Acts

OCCASION	PASSAGE
The first Jewish believers	2:1–13
The Samaritans	8:14–17
The Gentiles	10:44–48
The partially taught disciples in Ephesus	19:3–7

■ *Paul encountered disciples of John the Baptist,*
■ *who were unaware of the events of Pentecost.*
■ *When Paul explained the fullness of Jesus'*
■ *baptism, the disciples requested a new bap-*
■ *tism. Paul laid hands on them, and they*
■ *received the Spirit.*

PAUL'S PREACHING IN EPHESUS (19:8–12)

For two years Paul preached the gospel in Ephesus and throughout the province so that all "who lived in the province of Asia heard the word of the Lord."

Another aspect of Paul's ministry in Ephesus involved the miracles of God. Luke described these as being "extraordinary," which is something of an understatement. The people would take cloths which Paul had touched and carry them to the sick for healing. The people believed that cloths which had touched the apostle's body had healing efficiency, and Luke indicated that such was indeed the case.

This break with the synagogue in Ephesus marks a painful phase in the development of the church. From this point on, the break between Jews and Christians, between synagogue and church, widened rapidly.

- *For three months Paul pleaded and argued with the Ephesian Jews about the kingdom of God. However, they refused to believe Paul's message. For two more years, Paul preached the gospel in Ephesus and throughout the province of Asia.*

PAUL'S ENCOUNTER WITH FALSE RELIGION IN EPHESUS (19:13–20)

The example of Paul's genuine miracle working is followed by two episodes that involve false attempts to accomplish the miraculous.

Ephesus

One of the largest and most impressive cities in the ancient world and capital of the Roman province of Asia during the reign of Hadrian.

The city played a significant role in the expansion of Christianity.

At the time of Paul, Ephesus was probably the fourth largest city in the world with a population of 250,000.

There is one other aspect of Paul's Ephesian ministry that Luke did not elaborate on but which can be gleaned from Paul's letters. This was a period of extensive interaction with the churches which he had establised elsewhere. It was from Ephesus that Paul wrote his first letter to the Corinthians.

Ephesus was noted as a center of magic. The famous statue of Artemis, the centerpiece of her temple, was noted for the mysterious terms engraved on the crown, girdle, and feet of the image. Referred to as the "Ephesian scripts," this magical gibberish was considered to have great power.

Jewish Exorcists (vv. 13–16)

A group of fake exorcists who claimed to be sons of one Sceva, whom they declared to be a high priest (no such high priest ever existed, according to the best records), traveled around the empire, purportedly casting out demons. They watched Paul work and heard him casting out demons and do healing "in the name of Jesus."

They reasoned that if this worked for Paul, it would for them. The next time they confronted a man who seemed to be possessed by demons, they commanded the tormenting devils to come out "in the name of Jesus, whom Paul preaches."

The evil spirit answered them, "Jesus I know, and I know about Paul, but who are you?" Suddenly the possessed man leaped upon the seven scoundrels, beat them with superhuman strength, tore their clothes from their bodies, and sent them reeling naked into the streets of Ephesus.

Two lessons emerge from this story. First, Christianity has nothing to do with magic. The name of Jesus is no magical incantation. The power of Jesus drives out the demonic, and His Spirit only works through those who, like Paul, confess Him and are committed to Him. Second, the demon did confess the power of Jesus over Him.

Overcoming Magic (vv. 17–20)

This episode shows the triumph of the gospel over magic and the occult. To celebrate further the victory of Christian faith over magic, Luke recorded the memorable scene when many citizens of Ephesus who had practiced magic and soothsaying burned their books and completely forsook their attempts at the magical arts. Books were expensive items in those days, but books of magic would have commanded a handsome price. Luke estimated the value of those burned in Ephesus at fifty thousand pieces of silver.

PAUL'S DETERMINATION TO GO TO JERUSALEM (19:21–22)

Toward the end of his Ephesian ministry, Paul made a major decision. He determined to conclude his mission in the eastern provinces, go to Jerusalem, and then on to Rome.

OPPOSITION TO PAUL BY THE CRAFTSMAN OF EPHESUS (19:23–41)

Instigation of a Riot by Demetrius (vv. 23–27)

Paul and his friends had been so effective in the campaign to win the Roman province of Asia for Christ that many people had become believers, forsaking Artemis and her craftsmen in the process. Demetrius, apparently a leader among the silversmiths, became so agitated over the financial threat that he inflamed others in the craftsman's guild to a riotous protest against Paul and other Christian leaders.

Uproar in the Theater (vv. 28–34)

Demetrius's appeal had the desired effect, with all the craftsmen running forth and shouting, "Great is Artemis of the Ephesians." (Note that it was his appeal to religious and civic pride that was picked up.) A crowd quickly formed. Two of Paul's traveling companions from Macedonia were seized.

The mob then rushed into the theater, the largest public building in Ephesus. It was an open-air amphitheater, 495 feet in diameter, built into the western slope of Mt. Pion. Its seating capacity has been estimated at 24,500.

A man named Alexander moved before the crowd and motioned for silence to make a defense before the people.

Pacification by the City Clerk (vv. 35–41)

Alexander was not able to gain the crowd's attention. The city clerk, however, had no difficulty quieting the commotion.

The Greek Goddess Artemis

Artemis was the Greek goddess of the moon. She was the daughter of Zeus and Leto, whose worship was threatened by Paul's preaching of the gospel. Artemis was the goddess who watched over nature for both humans and animals. She was considered the great mother image who gave fertility to humankind. In the Greek homeland she was usually portrayed by the statues as a young, attractive virgin with her hair pulled back on her head wearing a short tunic. In Ephesus and Asia Minor she was portrayed as a more mature woman. Her robe was draped in such a way as to expose her bosom, which was covered with multiple breasts, depicting her gift of fertility and nurture.

He outlined the two primary legal avenues Demetrius and his fellow craftsman could follow if they had any grievances against the Christians. One was the provincial court conducted by the Roman proconsul on specific days. The other was the regular town assembly.

The clerk then clinched his argument. He told the Ephesians that they were running the danger of being charged with insurrection, since they really had no legally valid basis for their unruly behavior. The clerk's counsel carried the day. He dismissed the gathering and the crowd disappeared.

■ *This event indicates that Christians were not*
■ *seen as a threat to the state and that they*
■ *should be treated with tolerance in a reli-*
■ *giously pluralistic society. After the trouble*
■ *ceased, Paul left Ephesus for Macedonia.*

QUESTIONS TO GUIDE YOUR STUDY

1. What were the disciples of John lacking? How did Paul rectify the situation?
2. What lesson can we learn from the story about the sons of Sceva?
3. How did Paul escape the mob incited by Demetrius the silversmith? What evidences are there that God was in control of the events in Paul's life?

- - - - - - - - - - - - - - - -

PAUL'S FINAL MINISTRY IN MACEDONIA AND GREECE (20:1–6)

A Productive Visit to Greece (vv. 1–3a)

After traveling around in Greece (Achaia) for some months, he settled in Corinth for the winter months. Many scholars believe it was during these cold days of winter (A.D 56–57) that Paul wrote his great Epistle to the Romans, preparing the way for what he hoped would be a pastoral visit to the captial city of the Roman Empire.

While strengthening the church or churches in Corinth and doing his writing, Paul also coordinated the collection of the offering he wanted to take to Jerusalem to relieve the suffering of the Christians there.

Paul Eludes a Plot (vv. 3b–4)

Just as he was about to board what may have been a ship filled with Jewish pilgrims headed for worship in Jerusalem, Paul and his friends uncovered a plot on the apostle's life. Indications are that once at sea, Paul would have been murdered. Because plots were by now old hat, but never to be taken lightly, Paul changed his plans. He journeyed by land to Macedonia and sailed from there to Jerusalem.

The Rendezvous in Troas (vv. 5–6)

His traveling companions went on ahead of Paul to wait for him in Troas. Paul, who had evidently been joined by Luke, remained in Philippi until after the Passover before setting sail for the rendezvous in Troas.

After the season of Passover, Paul and Luke sailed for Troas where they stayed seven days in final

Paul's Companions

At this point, Paul was fortunate to have with him companions from a number of cities where he had ministered. Sopater from Berea; Aristarchus and Secundus from Thessalonica; Gaius from Derbe; Timothy from Lystra; Tychicus and Trophimus from Asia.

preparation for the trip to Jerusalem, which the resolute apostle felt compelled to make.

■ *Paul left Ephesus for a final swing through*
■ *Greece, back to Asia Minor, and finally to Jeru-*
■ *salem. After eluding a plot on his life, Paul*
■ *caught up with his traveling companions in*
■ *Troas.*

RESTORATION OF EUTYCHUS (20:7–12)

On their last day in Troas (a Sunday), Paul met with Christians for worship. This is one of the earliest references to Christians meeting for worship on Sunday.

Since he was leaving the next morning by ship, Paul spent all the time he could with the Christians in Troas, talking far into the night. Eutychus, a young believer, perhaps even a slave, sat listening in the window of the upper chamber in which Paul was speaking.

Eutychus had probably taken refuge in the window to catch a breath of fresh air to fight drowsiness. That effort, however, brought disastrous results. He fell asleep and tumbled from the third story to the ground.

The congregation rushed outside. The boy appeared dead from the fall. But Paul examined him, put his arm around him, and said, "Don't be alarmed, he's alive!" To everyone's amazement, the boy was still alive.

■ *As Paul preached into the wee hours of the*
■ *morning, Eutychus, a young believer, sat lis-*

■ *tening in a window of the upper chamber. He*
■ *fell asleep and tumbled from the third story*
■ *to the ground. Paul restored him back to*
■ *health.*

VOYAGE TO MILETUS (20:13–16)

At Assos, Paul boarded the coastal ship that skirted the rugged shoreline, putting in at major towns and cities along the route—a sort of "commuter" boat. Since he was attempting to reach Jerusalem by Pentecost, he decided not to go all the way to Ephesus. Instead, when the boat made port at Miletus, about thirty miles from Ephesus, he sent word to the city asking the leaders of the Christian community to come to Miletus.

PAUL'S FAREWELL ADDRESS TO THE EPHESIAN ELDERS (20:17–35)

Paul begins by reminding the Ephesians of his conduct, style of ministry, and devotion while he was among them.

Paul could honestly say that he did not value his life above the calling God had given him. What really mattered to him was to do the will of God, to answer His call to the fullest extent, and to do what the heavenly Father prepared him to do. To sum up his speech, Paul said, in effect, "I've done all I can for you. Now it's up to you."

Tucked away in this passage is a challenging statement. Paul could honestly say, "I have not hesitated to proclaim to you the whole will of God." Christian teachers must deliver the whole Word of God, the positive and the negative, the soothing and the corrective.

Verse 32 is a beautiful benediction. Paul commended his Ephesian friends to God and to the

This is an unusual passage (vv. 18–35) in that it is the only recorded address that Paul made to Christians. His other sermons were delivered either to Jews or Gentiles. This sermon contains both exhortation in the faith as well as defense (apology) of the faith. The sermon sounds very much like some of Paul's letters. It's likely that Luke actually heard the sermon, was deeply impressed by it, and in later years reconstructed the speech when he compiled Acts.

word of his grace, which was able to build them up and to bestow their full inheritance as members of the Christian community.

■ *Paul reported to the church about his mis-*
■ *sionary activity. His Miletus address is his*
■ *third and final speech in Acts during the*
■ *course of his missionary work.*

Paul's Missionary Speeches in Acts

LOCATION	MISSION	PASSAGE	AUDIENCE
Pisidian Antioch (synagogue)	First journey	13:16–41	Jews
Athens, Greece (Areopagus)	Second journey	17:22–31	Gentiles
Miletus	Third journey	20:17–35	Christians

FINAL LEAVE TAKING (20:36–38)

For all his brave talk about marching steadfastly to Jerusalem, when the final moment of parting came, Paul and the elders were overcome with sadness. Grown men knelt by the seashore, joined hands, prayed to their heavenly Father, and wept. Then, spent by years, yet profoundly encouraged by his words and example, those stalwart Ephesian leaders escorted Paul to his ship. With one more round of desperate, clinging embraces they put him on board and watched him sail away.

■ *This section concludes Paul's Ephesian minis-*
■ *try with its final farewell to the leaders of the*

■ *church. From this point on, the focus will*
■ *be Rome.*

QUESTIONS TO GUIDE YOUR STUDY

1. What did the resurrection of Eutychus mean to the Christians who witnessed this event?
2. In the opening statement of his farewell to the Ephesian elders, Paul offered a model for ministry. What are the elements of the model and how might we apply them to our present-day church ministries?
3. What are the key points of Paul's complete address to the Ephesian elders?

ACTS 21

VOYAGE TO JERUSALEM (21:1–16)
After the parting scene at Miletus, Paul resumed his final voyage to Jerusalem.

Warning at Tyre (vv. 1–6)
At Tyre, Paul and his traveling companions found the Christian community. Most likely it had been established by the Hellenist mission to Phoenicia mentioned in Acts 11:19. During his visit, the Tyrian Christians "through the Spirit" urged Paul not to go to Jerusalem.

Warning of Agabus (vv. 7–14)
Paul's next stopping point was Ptolemais, some twenty-five miles south of Tyre, the most southerly of the Phoenician ports.

Here, Agabus reenters Luke's narrative (see 11:27–30). In a symbolic act much like the acted-out prophecies of the Old Testament prophets, Agabus predicted Paul's coming

Agabus

Prophet in Jerusalem who visited the church at Antioch and predicted a universal famine. His prophecy was fulfilled about ten years later during the reign of Claudius Caesar.

arrest in Jerusalem. He took Paul's girdle, the long cloth wound several times around his waist, and bound his hands and feet with it. Then he gave the interpretation of the act. The prophecy was that Paul would be bound by the Jews of Jerusalem and handed over to the Gentiles.

Paul's Arrival in Jerusalem (vv. 15–16)

Paul's journey was now nearly complete. There remained only the final sixty-four miles between Caesarea and Jerusalem. The Caesarean Christians had made housing arrangements for Paul with a man named Mnason. The Christian community at Jerusalem gladly welcomed Paul and his colleagues.

En route to Jerusalem, Paul received warnings of the imprisonment and hardships that awaited him in Jerusalem.

THE PLAN OF THE JERUSALEM ELDERS (21:17–26)

After greeting the respected leaders of the church, Paul proceeded to tell them about all that God had done through him for the Gentiles. Paul did not owe these elders a report, but out of respect for their positions and the importance of the Jerusalem church, Paul was willing and eager to relate to them his experience as a missionary to the Gentiles.

Success was his problem. The elders rejoiced over his success—a genuine rejoicing, no doubt. They then shared their misgivings. Paul's success had stirred up some animosity among Jews in Jerusalem. In addition, lies had been spread about his work and regarding his views on Gentiles and circumcision, dietary laws, and the relinquishing of ancient Jewish traditions.

To offset the lies and to assure the orthodox Jews of Paul's Jewishness, the Christian elders had devised a plan. Paul would accompany to the temple four Jewish men who had taken a vow of purification and rededication. Paul would go through the same ritual of restoration they did and then pay the temple tax for them and himself. The process would take seven days. In this way the Jewish elders hoped the resentment among the orthodox Jews toward Paul would subside.

Paul agreed to this plan. He felt no inner need to go through the temple rituals. However, if it would keep peace in Jerusalem and give him further opportunity to preach to his Jewish brothers, he would attempt the reconciliation.

"Paul's Purification"

It was customary for Jews returning to Jerusalem from Gentile territories to undergo a purification ritual which lasted seven days. This demonstrated full loyalty to the Torah.

Paul underwent this purification and bore the heavy expense of doing so. He did not see his allegiance to Jesus as Messiah as at odds with his loyalty to the Torah.

■ *Paul's successful missionary work had*
■ *stirred up animosity among the orthodox*
■ *Jews in Jerusalem. To attempt a reconcilia-*
■ *tion with those Jews and assure them of his*
■ *Jewishness, Paul agreed to the elder's plan.*

THE RIOT AND PAUL'S ARREST IN THE TEMPLE AREA (21:27–36)

It was apparently the last day of the agreed-to plan of the elders when some Jews from Asia Minor screamed that Paul had brought Gentiles into the inner court of the temple and had, by doing so, defiled it. This false claim arose from the fact that Paul was seen in Jerusalem with a believer from Ephesus—Trophimus. The result of this was that the city was aroused. Immediately the crowd seized Paul, dragged him out of the temple area, and began to beat him. Meanwhile, word spread to the commander of the

Tower of Antonio

Roman soldiers were stationed at the Tower of Antonio, a fortress along the northwest corner of the wall that surrounded the Temple complex.

Roman forces in Jerusalem that the entire city was in confusion. The commander promptly moved to the eye of the storm with soldiers and officers. When the crowd saw the Romans approaching, they stopped beating Paul.

The Romans bound Paul with chains and pulled him away from the hostile crowd. The soldiers scurried up the steps into the fortress, dragging Paul with them.

■ *Jews from Asia Minor falsely accused Paul of*
■ *bringing a Gentile into the inner court of the*
■ *temple area and thereby incited a riot.*

PAUL'S REQUEST TO ADDRESS THE CROWD (21:37–40)

As the soldiers whisked Paul away, he, in the Greek language, asked permission to address the tribune. Astonished that his prisoner knew Greek, the tribune (commander) demanded, "Aren't you the Egyptian who started a revolt and led four thousand terrorists out into the desert some time ago?"

Paul answered, "No, I am a Jew, from Tarsus . . . Please let me speak to the people." Taken aback for a moment, the tribune motioned the crowd to be quiet and let Paul stand before them.

QUESTIONS TO GUIDE YOUR STUDY

1. What did Agabus's warning mean?
2. What plan did the Jerusalem Christians devise to reconcile Paul with the orthodox Jews. Why would it work?
3. Of what was Paul falsely accused? Why did this incident kill the elders' plan?

PAUL'S SPEECH BEFORE THE TEMPLE CROWD (22:1–21)

When Paul spoke in Hebrew, the crowd grew even quieter in order to hear everything he had to say. Paul began his speech by closely identifying with the Jews. Although not of Judah but a Jew nonetheless, Paul was educated under the esteemed Gamaliel, reared in the most orthodox manner. And Paul had vigorously attacked the new Christian movement when it appeared to be a threat to the ancient religion. Skillfully he retold his conversion experience on the Damascus road. In the next phase of his sermon he told of his command from the Lord to go to the Gentiles. With the mention of the Gentiles, the mob began to throw off their coats and toss dust in the air, shouting and calling for Paul's death.

■ *Paul began his defense by identifying himself*
■ *with his Jewish crowd. He told of his days as*
■ *a persecutor, then spoke of his conversion*
■ *and command to take the gospel to the Gen-*
■ *tiles. Before he could finish, he was cut off by*
■ *the Jewish mob.*

THE ATTEMPTED EXAMINATION BY THE TRIBUNE (22:22–29)

The narrative following Paul's address is extremely dramatic and filled with suspense. At first it looked as though Paul might be torn to shreds by the Jewish mob, but he was once again rescued by Lysias, the Roman tribune (commander), and taken safely into the barracks. But the tide turned against Paul again as

Claudius Lysias

Claudius Lysias was the Roman tribune or army captain who protected Paul from Jews who wanted to assassinate him. He helped Paul escape the Jews so he could appear before Felix, the governor.

Roman Citizenship

Roman citizenship rights were first formulated in the Valerian Law at the founding of the Roman Republic in 509 B.C., but citizenship rights changed as Roman governments changed. In New Testament times the definition of citizenship came in the Julian Law passed near 23 B.C.

Roman citizenship could be gained in several ways: birth to Roman parents, including birth to a Roman woman without regards to the identity of the father; retirement from the army; being freed from slavery by a Roman master; buying freedom from slavery; being given citizenship by a Roman general or emperor as an individual or as part of a political unit; purchase of citizenship. Paul was a born citizen, but how his family gained citizenship we do not know.

the tribune decided to examine him by the cruel Roman method of scourging. He was determined to flog Paul into some kind of confession. Again Paul was rescued—this time by an appeal to his Roman citizenship.

The tribune asked Paul, "Are you a Roman citizen?"

Paul answered, "Yes, I am." Those who were about to question Paul withdrew from him immediately. The tribune himself became alarmed when he realized that he had placed Paul, a Roman citizen, in chains. The tribune abandoned his plans to scourge Paul and decided to involve the Jewish authorities to help settle the issue.

■ *As Paul was being prepared for flogging and*
■ *questioning, he appealed to his Roman citi-*
■ *zenship. His questioners could not lawfully*
■ *harm a citizen of the Roman Empire.*
■ *Instead, the tribune decided to involve the*
■ *Jewish authorities to settle the matter.*

QUESTIONS TO GUIDE YOUR STUDY

1. What was Paul's message to the temple crowd? What particularly incited them?
2. How was Paul able to evade a flogging by claiming Roman citizenship?
3. Lysias, the Roman tribune, again saved Paul from the mob. What kind of impact do you believe Paul had on the life of this Roman commander?

PAUL BEFORE THE SANHEDRIN
(22:30–23:11)

Determined to know why the Jews would attack one of their own who was also a Roman citizen, the tribune arranged to have the Sanhedrin convene to hear Paul's case. Evidently, Rome's philosophy of governing her far-flung empire allowed each country to run its own affairs. Only in emergencies did Roman officials step in to have the final word. Lysias, the tribune, would have been content for the Jews to settle with Paul themselves so long as they did not violate his rights as a Roman citizen.

The Sanhedrin was an august body of influential Jews, but Paul was not intimidated by them. After all, he likely knew many of them from his days as a student of Gamaliel and his days as a persecutor of Christians. He did not hesitate to address the body as "brothers." But Paul's familiarity on the part of the accused along with his poise probably infuriated the high priest, Ananias. The high priest immediately ordered that Paul be struck on the mouth for blasphemy.

Paul's response is understandable: "God will strike you, you whitewashed wall."

When reprimanded for his insult, Paul said, "Brothers, I did not realize that he was the high priest." Paul may have said this with a tone of irony. In effect, Paul was saying, "He didn't act like a high priest; how could I recognize him as such when he was so totally out of character?"

At verse 6 the proceeding takes a radical turn. Paul saw the makeup of the group to be conservative Pharisees and liberal Sadducees, and he aligned himself with the Pharisees. He then

Ananias the High Priest

Ananias was the high priest of the Jewish court known as the Sanhedrin. This is the court that tried Paul in Acts 23. As was typical of high priests who belonged to the aristocratic Jewish group known as the Sadducees, he was concerned to appease Roman authorities and representatives. This desire may have prompted Ananias to take such a personal interest in Paul's case, especially since some Roman authorities suspected the apostle of sedition against Rome.

Because of Ananias's pro-Roman sentiments, he was assassinated by anti-Roman Jewish revolutionaries at the outbreak of the first great Jewish revolt against Rome in A.D 66.

stated what he saw as the real reason for the trial—his "hope in the resurrection of the dead." Immediately, both factions, always spoiling for a fight, began arguing vociferously. The dispute became so violent that the tribune became fearful for Paul's life. He commanded his officers to take Paul away.

The following night Paul was exhausted and fell into an uneasy sleep. Then came a sustaining vision of reassurance. Verse 11 says that "the Lord stood near Paul and said, 'Take courage! As you have testified about me in Jerusalem, so you must also testify in Rome.'" Now the visit to Jerusalem had received the Lord's endorsement.

Many of Paul's troubles the past two years had derived from his testifying to Christ before the Jews. Now his trip to Rome and all the legal hassle in between would be a testimony.

In the course of Paul's defense before the Sanhedrin, this body erupted into a violent discussion on the resurrection issue. The resurrection was the issue that separated Paul from the rest of the Jews. It was the real issue behind his trials, and in his subsequent defense speeches, Paul constantly insisted on that fact.

THE PLOT TO AMBUSH PAUL (23:12–22)

Paul had little rest. Forty or more fanatical Jewish zealots bound themselves by an oath neither to eat nor drink until Paul was dead. These vigilantes took the measure of their religious leaders and quickly decided their "spiritual mentors" would cooperate with the plot. The rulers were told to ask the tribune to bring Paul once again to the Sanhedrin so the case could be settled. But they planned to ambush Paul and the guard before they arrived to address the Sanhedrin.

But God was in control (vv. 16–22). At considerable personal risk, Paul's young nephew, who had learned of the plot secretly, informed Paul and ultimately the Roman tribune of the deeds that were being planned.

- *Paul's nephew uncovered a Jewish plot to kill*
- *Paul. This plot involved at least forty men*
- *and the Sanhedrin. Lysias, the tribune, was*
- *informed of the plot.*

PAUL IS HUSTLED TO CAESAREA (23:23–35)

Determined not to lose his Roman citizen prisoner at the hands of an assassination team, the tribune immediately called for two of his centurions. He ordered them to muster a large force of men to escort Paul out of the city under the cover of darkness. About nine o'clock at night Paul and his very large escort set out for the seacoast town of Caesarea.

Because of Paul's rank as a citizen and his reputation as a religious leader, Felix gave comfortable quarters within the palace, assuring him that the case would be heard as soon as possible.

- *Lysias, the tribune, had Paul escorted out of*
- *the city of Jerusalem under the cover of dark-*

Felix the Procurator

Antonius Felix was the procurator of Judea when Paul the apostle visited Jerusalem for the last time and was arrested there. He remained in office until A.D 60, when the emperor Nero recalled him. He was accused of poor administration.

Felix is depicted as a man who listened with interest to Paul's defense, but he failed to make any decision with regard to the case or to the personal implications of Paul's message. Rather, he hoped Paul would pay him a bribe. Contemporary historians paint Felix as a brutal, incompetent politician who was finally replaced.

■ *ness. Paul was delivered to Felix, the gover-*
■ *nor in Caesarea, for trial.*

QUESTIONS TO GUIDE YOUR STUDY

1. What was the significance of Paul's remark that Ananias the high priest was a "whitewashed wall"?

2. How does the story of the plot to ambush Paul show that God was in control of the events of Paul's life? To this point in Acts, how often did God use Roman officials to help or rescue Paul?

3. What kind of administrator was the Roman governor Felix? How did he handle Paul's case?

ACTS 24 · · · · · · · · · · · · · · ·

Structurally, Acts 24–26 is built around the three major political figures before whom Paul appeared—the procurators Felix and Festus and the Jewish King Agrippa II. In between comes the pivotal event of Paul's appeal to Caesar.

THE TRIAL IN CAESAREA (24:1–23)

The Charges (vv. 1–9)

With due ceremony, the high priest and some of his colleagues, accompanied by a professional prosecutor named Tertullus, arrived five days later. After attempting to ingratiate himself with the governor, Tertullus leveled three charges at Paul.

Members of the Sanhedrin all concurred in these charges.

Three Charges Against Paul

1. Paul was a pest in the empire who stirred up trouble everywhere.
2. He was a leader in the dangerous Nazarene sect.
3. He was a desecrater of the Temple in Jerusalem.

Paul's Rebuttal (vv. 10–21)

Paul then answered the charges against him. In his rebuttal he insisted he had not profaned the temple. Rather, he was quietly going through a process of purification when Jews from Asia Minor falsely accused him of defiling the temple. In fact, his behavior in Jerusalem was an example of true Jewish piety.

Paul did not deny, however, his involvement in the work of Christ. To the contrary, he gave a spirited testimony of the Way that had grown out of the Jewish religion. He insisted that he had not repudiated his commitment to the religion of his forebears when he took up the cause of Christ.

Felix's Indecision (vv. 22–23)

Felix quickly perceived that Paul had done nothing wrong, certainly nothing worthy of Roman punishment. But he knew that if he summarily acquitted Paul, the Jewish leaders would, stir up a riot and possibly murder Paul in the process. Under the guise of waiting to talk with the tribune, Lysias, Felix postponed a decision, thanked the Jewish rulers for their time, and ordered Paul placed under a rather loose house arrest.

■ *Paul's trial before Felix ended on an uncer-*
■ *tain note. Felix kept Paul in prison until the*
■ *end of his term of office.*

PAUL AND FELIX IN PRIVATE (24:24–27)

This concluding portion of Luke's treatment of Felix provides a glimpse into the procurator's personal life.

Why did Felix persist in calling in Paul for private conversations with him and his Jewish wife Drusilla? Obviously, Paul made both of them uncomfortable as he talked about justice, self-control, and future judgment. Still, they invited him on several occasions. It is true that Felix hoped for a bribe, but there must have been something in Paul's message that both attracted and repelled the regal couple.

- *Although Felix and his wife met privately*
- *with Paul on several occasions, they never*
- *fully believed his message of the gospel.*

QUESTIONS TO GUIDE YOUR STUDY

1. Tertullus the Jewish prosecutor leveled what three charges at Paul?

2. After hearing the charges brought against Paul, what decision did Felix render on the case?

3. Why do you think Felix was persistent in calling in Paul for private conversations with him and his Jewish wife Drusilla?

ACTS 25

Festus

Assumed his office at Nero's appointment in A.D. 60. He held the office until his death in 62.

FESTUS PRESSURED BY THE JEWS (25:1–5)

As a direct result of Jewish unrest, Felix was recalled to Rome and replaced by Porcius Festus. No sooner had he come to town than the Sanhedrin rulers began to apply pressure on the governor to let Paul come to Jerusalem for trial.

These wily elders sought to take advantage of the inexperienced governor.

Perhaps Felix had briefed Festus on the Paul issue, or Festus may simply have refused to be stampeded into any action he would later regret. Instead, he invited a representative group to accompany him back to Caesarea, where together they would confront Paul and attempt disposition of the case.

- *Recalled to Rome after an unsuccessful stint*
- *as procurator, Felix was replaced by Porcius*
- *Festus. Immediately the Sanhedrin rulers*
- *began pressuring Festus to bring Paul to*
- *Jerusalem for trial. Instead, Festus invited*
- *the officials to return with him to Caesarea.*

PAUL'S APPEAL TO CAESAR (25:6–12)

The entire case had to be reopened to brief the new governor. Once again, the spokesman for the Sanhedrin hurled his empty charges at Paul while offering no proof for their validity. Paul calmly refuted every accusation.

This appeal was the right of every Roman citizen, although by no means did every citizen in trouble with local law get the privilege of journeying to Rome for a hearing.

Then the new governor gave the situation an unexpected (and providential) turn. Attempting to gain favor with the Jews, Festus asked Paul if he would be willing to go to Jerusalem for a full trial before the Sanhedrin. Paul knew he would have a better chance in a den of hungry lions than in Jerusalem.

Paul's response: "I appeal to Caesar!"

With Paul's appeal, Festus was suddenly off the hook.

"You have appealed to Caesar. To Caesar you will go!" declared Festus.

- *Realizing that he would receive fairer treat-*
- *ment before the emperor in Rome than before*
- *the Sanhedrin in Jerusalem, Paul exercised*
- *his right as a Roman citizen and appealed to*
- *Caesar. Happy to be rid of Paul, Festus*
- *granted Paul's appeal.*

Agrippa II

Son of Agrippa I and brother of Drucilla and Bernice. With Agrippa II's death the Herodian dynasty came to an end in title as well as in fact.

FESTUS'S CONVERSATION WITH AGRIPPA (25:13–22)

Within days of Paul's appeal, Festus received a visit from the Jewish King Agrippa II and his sister Bernice. Likely this was an official visit to establish relationships with the new procurator upon his assumption of office. As king of the Jews, Festus felt that King Agrippa was in a unique position to assist him in the matter of Paul's appeal.

He told Agrippa that the Jews raised none of the charges "which [he] expected." This most likely meant that the Jews were not able to charge Paul with treason or any crime under Roman law. Festus concluded his account by informing Agrippa of Paul's appeal. He was now holding Paul until he could arrange his transmittal to Caesar. In courteous language, Agrippa replied he would like to hear Paul himself. Festus granted his request.

- *Festus felt that King Agrippa could assist*
- *him in the matter of Paul's appeal. He needed*

- *to formulate an official report of the charges*
- *against Paul to be sent with the appeal.*

PAUL BEFORE AGRIPPA: THE SETTING (25:23–27)

Festus set forth the immediate agenda, which was something definite he could place in his report to the emperor. He himself was at a loss for any specific charges they could level against Paul. He considered sending a prisoner to Rome without charges "unreasonable." He asked for Agrippa's assistance because the king was more familiar with Jewish matters.

"Unreasonable"

The Greek word literally means "senseless." The charges against Paul were completely without foundation.

- *The importance of Paul's coming address is*
- *underlined by all the pageantry of the nota-*
- *bles parading into the audience chamber.*
- *Because he had no specific charges against*
- *Paul, he called on King Agrippa for assis-*
- *tance. As it turned out, Festus was not a ster-*
- *ling example of Roman justice.*

QUESTIONS TO GUIDE YOUR STUDY

1. How did the new governor, Festus, attempt to handle Paul's case?
2. What conclusions did Festus and Agrippa come to as a result of their conversation?
3. Why did Festus request Agrippa's assistance?

ACTS 26

Paul's speech before Agrippa is the culmination of Paul's defense in chapters 21–26. It brings together in final form all the themes of the previous five chapters.

PAUL'S ADDRESS BEFORE AGRIPPA (26:1–23)

This speech before Agrippa is strikingly parallel to Paul's speech before the temple mob. On both occasions Paul gave a testimony of his personal experience in Christ: his Jewish upbringing; his persecution of the Jews; his conversion; and his commission from the risen Lord.

With great ceremony and pageantry, the lords and ladies of the city gathered in the courtroom with Festus, King Agrippa and his sister Bernice, and certain Jewish leaders to hear Paul's defense. When Festus had done his sonorous intonings, Agrippa gave Paul permission to speak.

Paul declared he was glad for the opportunity to state his case before the knowledgeable king. Although always pro-Roman, Agrippa had a Jewish background that probably gave him some acquaintance with Jewish religious and political maneuverings. Thus he could listen with some appreciation to Paul's defense.

Once again Paul retold his conversion experience on the Damascus road. Notice that each time Paul tells the story (or Luke records the telling) different shades of the narrative appear, but always there is the consistent theme: his determination to harass Christians, the great light, the voice, the blindness, and the total redirection of Paul's life.

Paul closed by saying that he had been obedient to his vision of Christ. He closed by testifying that his life had been a witness for Christ.

- Paul once again appeared before a Roman
- official—this time King Agrippa. Again he
- emphasized his innocence of any breach of

■ *Roman law. Each of his trials brought him a*
■ *step closer to Rome, and with each step he*
■ *presented his testimony of Jesus.*

PAUL'S APPEAL TO AGRIPPA (26:24–29)

Paul's talk about the Jewish Scripture and his references to the Resurrection became too much for the Roman procurator. Festus interrupted Paul's address with, "You are out of your mind, Paul! Your great learning is driving you insane." Although showing a popular prejudice often directed toward scholars, Festus did show a genuine respect for Paul's learning.

Respectfully, Paul asserted he was in possession of his faculties. Then he directed an appeal to the king: "King Agrippa, do you believe the prophets? I know you do." In effect, Paul was saying, "King, you know what I am talking about; you are alert. These marvelous events have not taken place in a tiny corner. The gospel is exploding all over the empire, especially in your kingdom." Suddenly the king was the defendant!

"In a Corner"

What had taken place was not done in secret, as was sometimes charged, but was done in the open, a matter of public knowledge.

Agrippa protested with alarm. "Do you think that in such a short time you can persuade me to be a Christian?"

In a final burst of testimony, Paul declared, "Short time or long—I pray God that not only you but all who are listening to me today may become what I am, except for these chains." As a follower of Jesus Christ, Paul considered himself a free man in spite of the chains he was wearing.

PAUL'S INNOCENCE DECLARED BY GOVERNOR AND KING (26:30–32)

All this was too much for the royal inquisitors. Quickly the king and his sister, along with the governor, swept out of the courtroom. Safely in the governor's chambers, the king and Festus agreed there was no legitimate charge against Paul. If he had not appealed to Caesar, he could have been freed. But history's question to them is, in the face of Jewish opposition, *would* they have freed Paul?

■ *After speaking to Paul, even Agrippa declared*
■ *his innocence. In all, three times Paul appeared*
■ *before Roman officials; each time no official*
■ *verdict was rendered. Paul was about to realize*
■ *his desire to preach the gospel in Rome.*

QUESTIONS TO GUIDE YOUR STUDY

1. What did Paul's defense sermons emphasize?
2. Describe Paul's appeal to King Agrippa. What can we make of Agrippa's response?
3. What did the governor and the king declare about Paul's guilt or innocence?

ACTS 27

Most of the concluding two chapters of Acts is devoted to an extensive narrative of Paul's journey by sea from Caesarea to Rome to appear before Caesar. The account has much in common with ancient sea narratives and has provoked a lively discussion among scholars. The route followed, the landmarks passed, and the time lapse are all given considerable detail. Likewise, there is a heavy use of technical seafaring terminology, and the account is considered a valuable source for ancient sailing techniques by scholars of the history of navigation.

The extensive travel narrative is one long, continuous story, and any division is somewhat arbitrary. The structure, however, does seem to involved an interplay with scenes that focus on Paul.

PAUL'S JOURNEY TO FAIR HAVENS (27:1–8)

As soon as Festus had agreed to Paul's appeal to Caesar, arrangements were made for Paul and some other prisoners to be transported to Rome under the supervision of a centurion of the select Augustan Cohort. Luke accompanied Paul on this voyage. From the seaport of Caesarea, the band of prisoners, their guards, and other passengers took passage on a coastal ship that would put in at the small harbors along the way. The centurion's aim was to sail on this smaller vessel until he could arrange booking on a trans-Mediterranean ship.

After several weeks of slow travel, the desired passage was secured, and the centurion and his group boarded what was probably a large grain ship headed for Rome. The sailing season was getting shorter. The most advantageous time for sailing was late spring and summer. Indications are that it was early fall, which always brought uncertain winds making for slow, erratic sailing. In a harbor of Crete called Fair Havens, a shipboard conference was held with the centurion, the shipowner-captain, and Paul attending. Should they put in here for the winter or attempt to reach a more desirable harbor? Paul, from his years of experience as a traveler, urged them to stop where they were. The centurion

Paul's Journey to Rome

Note the appearance again of the "we" sections of Acts. Luke, the author of Acts, joined Paul for this trip to Rome and remained with him until Paul was delivered into the custody of soldiers in Rome (28:16).

The journey to Rome involved typical navigational practices and patterns of the first century. Due to dangerous weather conditions, no sailing occurred in the Mediterranean Sea during the period from mid-November to early March. Paul's voyage was near the beginning of this dangerous period, and the trip to Rome was interrupted by the advent of a sudden storm known as the "Euraquilo," a term for the northwest wind. The gale blew the ship for two weeks before it struck a reef at the island of Malta and broke apart.

and captain, however, wanted to push on to a safer harbor. Paul predicted that the voyage would be dangerous to both ship and life, but his warning was not heeded.

■ *Paul and some other prisoners were to be*
■ *transported to Rome under the supervision of*
■ *a centurion of the select Augustan Cohort. In*
■ *a harbor of Crete called Fair Havens, the cen-*
■ *turion in charge and the vessel's sailing pro-*
■ *fessionals decided to push on to a safer harbor*
■ *in spite of Paul's prediction that the voyage*
■ *would be dangerous.*

THE DECISION TO SAIL ON (27:9–20)

The decision to sail having been made, Paul and his party still had to wait for a favorable wind, that was not long in coming. No doubt with lumps in their throats, the crew headed the ship for the open sea. For a short time all went well, but suddenly a devastating northeastern wind came roaring upon them without warning. Since it was impossible to sail into the wind, the captain was forced to let the ship scud before the gale. After days of this kind of maddening sailing, they managed to put into a harbor of sorts at Clauda where they lashed the ship with cables to strengthen the hull. Back into the sea they were driven by the winds, but the storm did not abate. The ship's cargo and gear were gradually thrown overboard in an effort to make the ship more stable in the tossing sea. After days in the storm, the crew and passengers began to despair of coming through alive.

"Undergirders"

Ancient ships had as part of their ordinary gear, undergirders which were simply ropes for passing round the hull of a ship. This practice helped prevent leaking when the ship was tossed in a storm.

■ *The ship encountered a northeastern wind*
■ *that made sailing nearly impossible. In spite*
■ *of the crew's efforts, the ship lost time, the*
■ *conditions worsened, and sailing became*
■ *more dangerous. Those aboard began to fear*
■ *for their lives.*

PAUL'S WORD OF ASSURANCE (27:21–26)

During all these days and nights no one had eaten anything. Who could even think of food while they fought every minute just to stay alive? Then one morning, Paul stood up, clung to a mast or a line, and declared: "Men, you should have taken my advice not to sail from Crete.... But ... keep up your courage, because not one of you will be lost." Paul told them that he had had a dream the previous night and was assured that even though the ship and cargo were in danger, there would be no loss of life.

THE PROSPECT OF LANDING (27:27–32)

On the fourteenth night of this incredible journey, the sailors sensed they were nearing land. Soundings proved them right They were drifting toward some unknown island. To slow down the drift, they put out stern anchors. Under the pretense of laying out anchors, some of the ship's crew tried to get into the lifeboat, but Paul warned the centurion, "Unless these men stay with the ship, you cannot be saved." The soldiers promptly cut the rope that tethered the small dinghy to the ship. They were now literally "all in the same boat."

"Anchors were used as brakes and were normally cast from the bow. Here they are cast from the stern, as was occasionally done if the events would otherwise blow the ship around."

Craig S. Keenes in *The IVP Bible Background Commentary* Downers Grove: InterVarsity Press, 1993, p. 403.

PAUL'S' FURTHER ENCOURAGEMENT (27:33–38)

At the height of the storm, when spirits were at their lowest ebb, Paul had spoken words of reassurance. With the thwarted attempt of the sailors, a ship badly battered by the storm, and no assurance they could get it safely to shore, Paul again rose to encourage the shaky voyagers.

It was just before the break of day, and daylight would bring the rescue attempt. He urged everyone to eat some food, as they would need all the physical stamina they could muster just to survive. He reassured all aboard that none of them would "lose a single hair" from their heads. He then gave thanks before they ate.

■ *Paul further reassured the ship's crew and*
■ *passengers that they would survive their*
■ *ordeal at sea.*

THE DELIVERANCE OF ALL (27:39–44)

Final preparations for beaching the ship were made, only to have their plans dashed when it ran aground at her bow, leaving the stern exposed to the battering of the waves. The ship began to break up.

On instinct, the guards drew their swords to kill the prisoners lest they escape, but the centurion stopped them and allowed all the people, prisoners included, to get to shore the best way they could. By clinging to floating debris or swimming valiantly, everyone made it to safety, fulfilling Paul's prediction.

Paul's presence was in no sense responsible for the storm. If his advice had been followed, the ship would never have encountered the storm in the first place. On the contrary, Paul's presence was responsible for their deliverance from the storm. His God was with him, and because he was with the apostle, all were saved.

QUESTIONS TO GUIDE YOUR STUDY

1. Discuss the "we" sections that have appeared throughout Acts. What might Luke have tried to convey with these sections?

2. From their experience sailing with Paul during the voyage to Rome, what might the ship's crew and passengers have learned?

3. In the midst of a storm that lasted for days, Paul remained an encouragement to those around him. How might we apply this attitude to the "storms" we face in our own lives?

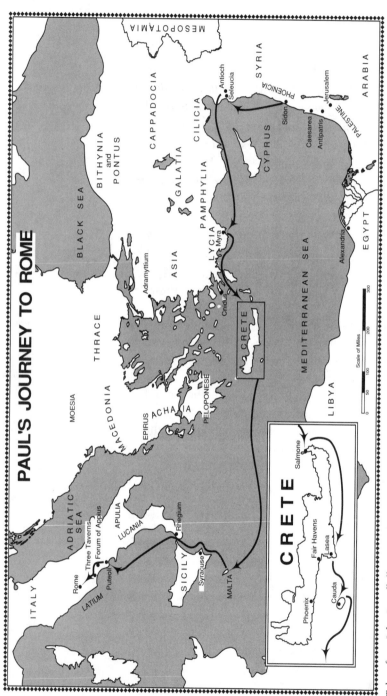

PAUL'S JOURNEY TO ROME

Taken from John B. Polhill, *Acts*, vol. 26, New American Commentary (Nashville, Tenn.:Broadman & Holman Publishers, 1992), p. 61.

ACTS 28

WINTERING IN MALTA (28:1–10)

In the dawn's early light, natives on the island looked out to the tossing sea and were surprised to see the ship breaking up with its frightened crew jumping overboard, swimming, clinging to planks, struggling toward land. By the time the shivering, bedraggled men stumbled to the beach, a big fire was blazing. They hovered around it, shaking from fear and cold. The island was Malta, off the southern coast of Italy. Luke remembered with deep appreciation the hospitality of the residents of that place.

Paul's Deliverance from the Viper (vv. 1–6)

To keep the fire going, and probably to get his own circulation moving, Paul stirred around the beach, gathering wood to toss on the fire. Evidently, he picked up a snake, a viper, in some brush, and the fire jarred the snake into activity. To the horror of all bystanders (and probably Paul), the poisonous snake suddenly struck Paul's hand. The natives concluded that Paul was a murderer who was being punished by the gods for his evil deeds. But to their amazement Paul suffered no ill effects. After shaking the snake into the fire, he went about seeing to the ship's company. The natives' fear quickly turned to awe as the supposed criminal turned out to be a "god."

The Hospitality of Publius (vv. 7–10)

The governor of the island, a man named Publius, invited Paul, the ship's captain, the centurion, and others among the group to his home. There he entertained them for three days. In the course of the visit, Paul was able to heal Publius's father of fever and dysentery as well as help many others on the island. After three months,

"St. Paul's Bay, in Malta with its little island creek and two seas meeting, fulfills all the conditions of Luke's narrative."
A.T. Robertson
Epochs in the Life of Paul, p. 263.

Luke used a word for snake that is the term for "viper." The viper is a poisonous snake, but it has been pointed out that there are no poisonous snakes on Malta today. The poisonous snake in this passage has provoked much discussion among scholars. Obviously, the current situation on the island would have little to say about conditions there in the first century. Obviously, the inhabitants of Malta recognized the viper as poisonous otherwise they wouldn't have reacted as they did.

the weather grew dependable enough for the group to continue their journey to Rome. Before they left, however, the people of Malta, out of gratitude for their healing and preaching, showered Paul, Luke, and the others with gifts for their voyage.

■ *After shipwrecking on Malta, Paul and his*
■ *group spent the next three months with the*
■ *people of that island. Paul was able to minis-*
■ *ter to them by healing the governor's father*
■ *and others.*

Puteoli

Puteoli, from its trade with Alexandria and the East must have had a colony of Jews who were related to the Jews in Rome. Also, they had a Christian community.

For some reason, the centurion allowed Paul (probably with a guard) to remain in Puteoli for seven days, during which he and the Christian community there became fast friends and enjoyed a time of mutual deepening of faith.

ROME AT LAST! (28:11–16)

In early February, passage was booked on a grain ship that had wintered in Malta. They sailed first to the port of Syracuse on the island of Sicily, then on to Rhegium in Italy, and finally to Puteoli in the Bay of Naples.

"And so we came to Rome" (v. 14)! What an understatement! For years Paul had wanted to come to Rome. He had written them his great Roman Epistle three years before. He had prayed to see Roman Christians face to face. At long last, after years in prison in Caesarea and one of the most harrowing sea voyages on record, he came to Rome.

Word of his arrival preceded Paul. Imagine his delight and gratitude when he was greeted at two towns along the way by groups of Christians from Rome, some walking as much as forty miles down the Appian Way to greet and make welcome their famous visitor. If the apostle harbored any fears, the sight of those brethren must have completely dispelled them. With tears and embracing, Paul and Luke greeted them. No matter that Paul was a prisoner bound for an uncertain future before Roman courts; he was in the hands of God, and the believers were delighted to meet him and have him in their midst. Once in Rome, Paul was again placed under house arrest with freedom to move about within the confines of the residence but without the liberty to leave. Some texts suggest he was lightly chained to a single guard—hence the chains mentioned in verse 20.

■ *For years Paul had wanted to come to Rome.*
■ *He had written them his great Roman epistle*
■ *three years before. He had prayed to see*
■ *Roman Christians face to face. At last, after*
■ *years in prison in Caesarea and one of the*
■ *most harrowing sea voyages on record, he*
■ *came to Rome.*

PAUL AND THE ROMAN JEWS (28:17–29)

After three days for rest and recuperation, he asked leaders of the Roman Jewish community to come to his residence for conversations. During their visit he explained to them the reasons for his imprisonment. When all the facts were considered, he declared that he was really a prisoner in Rome because of the "hope of Israel." His devotion to the ancient dreams of Israel—of a Messiah and God's intention of a universal brotherhood of believers—had cost him his freedom.

The Jews assured him they had received no communication from Jerusalem about him, and that must have been a relief to Paul. But even more important was their expressed desire to

"And now I am standing trial for the hope of the promise made by God to our fathers. The promise to which our twelve tribes hope to attain as they earnestly serve God night and day."
Acts 26:6–7, NASB

hear more from Paul about the Christian faith, which was gaining momentum in the Gentile world, although it was still terribly maligned by the Jews. All Paul wanted was an opportunity to preach to them.

On the appointed day, a large crowd of Jews gathered at Paul's house. From early morning until late evening he explained the kingdom of God as expressed in Jesus Christ. As he had done all over Asia Minor, he attempted to convince them that Christianity was not a competitor with but a fulfillment of Judaism. The response was typical—some believed and some did not. Apparently to set the record straight, the apostle told the crowd that he was not surprised at the mixed response, because the prophet Isaiah long ago had foretold that many of the very ones to whom the Messiah would be sent would reject Him. But that would not be the end of the matter. God's salvation had been sent also to the Gentiles, and they would listen.

And He said, "Go, and tell this people:
'Keep on listening, but do not perceive;
Keep on looking, but do not understand.'

Render the hearts of this people insensitive, Their ears dull,
And their eyes dim,
Lest they see with their eyes,
Hear with their ears,
Understand with their hearts,
And return and be healed."
Isa. 6:9–10, NASB

AN EPILOGUE WITHOUT A CONCLUSION (28:30–31)

For two years, at his own expense, Paul lived and preached in Rome, welcoming all who came to him. Acts comes to a rather abrupt ending. We ache to have a definitive answer about what happened to Paul after the two years. Was he executed? Was he freed? Did he make the trip to Spain that he had envisioned? We do not know. Whatever may have been the outcome of Paul's Roman imprisonment, Luke seems to have deliberately chosen to end the story in this abrupt way.

But of this we are sure: Paul preached the unsearchable riches of Jesus Christ openly and unhindered. During those years he wrote his famous "prison epistles," always concerned for persons and churches that were trying to live out the meaning of their faith in Christ. The content of Paul's message forms the conclusion to the Book of Acts. He preached "the kingdom of God" and taught about "the Lord Jesus Christ." The two belong together: the good news of the kingdom *is* the good news about Christ.

The Book of Acts ends as though there would be a sequel, and that has always been the spirit of the Church and the gospel. Thanks be unto God—the story has no end but moves on "unhindered."

For two years, at his own expense, Paul lived and preached in Rome, welcoming all who wanted to come to him. Then Acts comes to a rather abrupt ending. We do not know the outcome of Paul's Roman imprisonment. We do know that he preached the message of Jesus Christ openly and unhindered, and during those years wrote his famous "prison epistles."

QUESTIONS TO GUIDE YOUR STUDY

1. What did Paul accomplish in his three months on the island of Malta?
2. The Maltese people were lavish in their hospitality toward Paul and the others. Compare the reception from these pagan people with receptions he received from the many Jewish communities he visited.
3. What do we know about Paul's time in Rome? What do you think happened to Paul?

Paul's Missionary Journeys Harmonized with the Pauline Epistles

DATE	EPISTLE	EVENT
A.D. 29	Acts	Death and Resurrection of Christ.
A.D. 32	Acts	Conversion of Paul, followed by three-year period of preaching in Damascus and Arabia. Escaped a Jewish death plot in Damascus by being lowered over wall in city.
A.D. 32	Acts	Barnabas introduced Paul to Jerusalem church.
A.D. 32	Acts	Paul returned to Tarsus.
A.D. 32	Acts	Barnabas brought Paul to Syrian Antioch. Both took famine relief to Jerusalem.
A.D. 47	Acts	I. FIRST MISSIONARY JOURNEY Syrian Antioch Cyprus—Blinding of Elymas and conversion of proconsul Sergius Paulus.
A.D. 47	Acts	Perga—Departure of John Mark. Pisidian Antioch—Paul turned to Gentiles after preaching in synagogue.
A.D. 47	Acts	Iconium—Driven from the city after preaching in synagogue.

DATE	EPISTLE	EVENT
A.D. 47	Acts	Lystra—After Paul healed a cripple, crowd tried to worship Barnabas and Paul as Zeus and Hermes. Paul was stoned.
A.D. 47	Acts	Derbe
		Lystra
		Iconium
		Pisidian Antioch
		Perga
		Attalia
		Syrian Antioch
A.D. 49	Galatians (under south Galatia theory)	Jerusalem council (Acts 15)
A.D. 50–52	Galatians (under south Galatia theory)	II. SECOND MISSIONARY JOURNEY
		Antioch in Syria
		Derbe
		Lystra—Paul took Timothy (Acts 16:1)
A.D. 50–52	Galatians (under south Galatia theory)	Iconium
		Pisidian Antioch
		Troas—Paul received Macedonian vision.
		Philippi—Conversion of Lydia and exorcism of demon-possessed girl.
A.D. 50–52	Galatians (under south Galatia theory)	Jailing of Paul and Silas. Earthquake at midnight. Conversion of jailer.
A.D. 50–52	Galatians (under south Galatia theory)	Thessalonica—Paul driven from city by mob attack on Jason's house.
A.D. 50–52	Galatians (under south Galatia theory)	Berea—Jews listened to Paul's message and searched Old Testament to verify it.

DATE	EPISTLE	EVENT
A.D. 50–52	Galatians (under south Galatia theory)	Athens—Paul preached sermon on Hill of Ares (Mar's Hill).
A.D. 50–52	1 and 2 Thessalonians	Corinth—Paul involved in tentmaking with Priscilla and Aquila.
A.D. 50–52	1 and 2 Thessalonians	Conversion of Crispus, the synagogue ruler.
A.D. 50–52	1 and 2 Thessalonians	Paul remained one-and-a-half years in Corinth after the Roman governor Gallio refused to condemn his preaching.
A.D. 50–52	1 and 2 Thessalonians	Cenchrea—Paul took a Nazarite vow by shaving his head.
A.D. 50–52	1 and 2 Thessalonians	Ephesus—Left Priscilla and Aquila behind here.
A.D. 50–52	1 and 2 Thessalonians	Caesarea
		Jerusalem
		Syrian Antioch
A.D. 53–57	1 and 2 Thessalonians	III. THIRD MISSIONARY JOURNEY
		Syrian Antioch
		Galatia and Phrygia (Derbe, Lystra, Iconium, Pisidian Antioch).
A.D. 53–57	1 Corinthians	Ephesus—Preaching in school of Tyrannus. Converts renounced the occult by burning magical books. Demetrius led riot of silversmiths on behalf of goddess Artemis (Diana). Paul ministered for three years (20:31).
A.D. 53–57	2 Corinthians	Macedonia (Philippi, Thessalonica).

DATE	EPISTLE	EVENT
A.D. 53–57	Romans	Greece (Athens and Corinth)—Jews plotted to kill Paul on voyage to Palestine.
A.D. 53–57	Romans	Macedonia Troas—Healing of Eutychus after a fall from window during Paul's sermon.
A.D. 53–57	Romans	Miletus—Farewell to Ephesian elders.
A.D. 53–57	Romans	Tyre—Paul warned to avoid Jerusalem.
A.D. 53–57	Romans	Caesarea—Agabus warned Paul of suffering in Jerusalem.
A.D. 53–57	Romans	Jerusalem—Jews rioted against Paul in temple. He was rescued and arrested by Roman soldiers. Defended himself before Sanhedrin. Sent to Felix in Caesarea.
A.D. 53–57	Romans	Caesarea—Paul defended himself before Felix, Festus, and Agrippa. He appealed to trial in Rome.
A.D. 53–57	Romans	IV. JOURNEY TO ROME Crete—Paul advised sailors not to sail onto Mediterranean. Storm hit ship in which Paul was traveling.
A.D. 53–57	Romans	Malta—Paul's ship wrecked. Paul and companions remained here during winter.

DATE	EPISTLE	EVENT
A.D. 61	Philemon Colossians Ephesians Philippians	Rome—Paul is housed in a rented home. Preached to Jews and Gentiles. Waited two years for trial before Nero.
A.D. 63	1 Timothy Titus	Release from prison. Ministry in the east.
A.D. 67	2 Timothy	Reimprisonment.
A.D. 67	2 Timothy	Martyrdom.

Taken from Lea, Thomas D., *The New Testament: Its Background and Message* (Broadman & Holman Publishers: Nashville, Tenn.), pp. 304–08.

The following list is a collection of the sources works used for this volume. All are from Broadman & Holman's list of published reference resources: to accommodate the reader's need for more specific information and or for an expanded treatment of the Book of Acts. All of these works will greatly aid in the reader's study, teaching, and presentation of Luke's narrative of the Acts of the Apostles. The accompanying annotations can be helpful in guiding the reader to the proper resources.

RESOURCES:

Adams, J. McKee (revised by Joseph A. Callaway), *Biblical Backgrounds*. This work provides valuable information on the physical and geographical settings of Acts. Its many color maps and other features add depth and understanding to Luke's narrative.

Cate, Robert L., *A History of the New Testament and Its Times*. An excellent and thorough survey of the birth and growth of the Christian faith in the first-century world.

Holman Bible Dictionary. An exhaustive, alphabetically arranged resource of Bible-related subjects. An excellent tool of definitions and other information on the people, places, things, and events of the Bible.

Holman Bible Handbook, pp. 632–672. A comprehensive treatment of the Acts of the Apostles that offers outlines, commentary on key themes and sections, and full-color photos, illustrations, charts, and maps. Provides an accent on the broader theological teachings. Various selections were used throughout the Book of Acts.

Holman Book of Biblical Charts, Maps, and Reconstructions, pp. 99, 100. A colorful, visual collection of charts, maps, and reconstructions, These well-designed tools are invaluable to the study of the Bible.

Lea, Thomas D., *The New Testament: Its Background and Message*, pp. 281–29. An excellent resource for background material—political, cultural, historical, and religious. Provides background information in broad strokes on specific books, including the Gospels.

Maddox, Robert L., Jr., *Acts* (Layman's Bible Book Commentary). A popular-level treatment of the Book of Acts. This easy-to-use volume provides a relevant and practical perspective for the reader.

Polhill, John B., *Acts* (The New American Commentary), vol. 26. A more scholarly treatment of the text of Acts that provides emphases on the text itself, background, and theological considerations.

Robertson, A. T., *A Grammar of the Greek New Testament in the Light of Historical Research*. An exhaustive, scholarly work on the underlying language of the New Testament. Provides advanced insights into the grammatical, syntactical, and lexical aspects of the New Testament.